James Madison Goodhue

Struck a Lead

An Historical Tale of the upper Lead Region

James Madison Goodhue

Struck a Lead
An Historical Tale of the upper Lead Region

ISBN/EAN: 9783337025977

Printed in Europe, USA, Canada, Australia, Japan

Cover: Foto ©ninafisch / pixelio.de

More available books at **www.hansebooks.com**

STRUCK A LEAD.

AN HISTORICAL TALE OF THE UPPER LEAD REGION,

BY

JAMES M. GOODHUE,
Founder of the St. Paul Pioneer Press.

JOSEPH COVER, Jr., Publisher.

CHICAGO:
JAMESON & MORSE, 162-164 CLARK STREET.
1883.

Copyright, 1883,
BY
JOSEPH COVER, LANCASTER, WISCONSIN.

IN the following admirable series of sketches of life in the lead mines as it existed in the early days of the development of the lead industry in southwestern Wisconsin and northwestern Illinois, Col. Goodhue has woven both fact and fancy. He was for a time a resident of the locality wherein the scenes of the story are located, and partook of the pioneer life of the West as it then existed. His familiarity with the rugged and unique characters of that day has given his pen an easy grace in describing them; some of whom had their living prototypes in "the mines." Jim White was no imaginary Texan Major, nor did he consult imaginary lawyers.

The action in "forcible entry and detainer," and the omnibus bill passed by the Wisconsin Legislature, as herein depicted, are "studies from life," in the history of the Northwest.

Believing that Struck a Lead will have special interest to the early settlers of the lead district yet living, and to the many admirers of the brilliant author in his life time, as well as to the general reader, who will find delight in the romantic episodes that occur in "the wooing o't" between the hero and heroine,—this tale is herewith submitted to the public for the first time in book form, by

THE PUBLISHER.

STRUCK A LEAD.

AN HISTORIC TALE OF THE UPPER LEAD REGION.

CHAPTER I.

A MISSISSIPPI STEAMBOAT.

At sunset, on the 1st day of September, 184—, the steamboat Roarer, then lying at the port of St. Louis, cast off her moorings and swept gracefully into the channel of the Mississippi; and now she breasts the torrent with her strong arms, and dashes behind her a shower of spray, in which she is wreathed a moving rainbow. St. Louis, with her warehouses, steeples and steamboats, soon disappears in the distance, and the chiming of her evening bells break indistinctly upon the ears of the passengers, while the sun sinks, like a red iron ball, behind the wide plains of the West. The Roarer soon passes the mouth of the Missouri—which rushes down from the Rocky Mountains like a herd of affrighted buffaloes scampering through one of Cooper's novels (no libel intended)—and next she passes the city of Alton, reposing on the dusky bank of the river; Alton, the city of magnificent projects and bankrupt pork merchants; one of those mushroom cities which grew out of the expansion of bank issues in the years of 1835-36, and which was designed to be the focus of five hundred railroads, ENACTED by the Legislature of Illinois. Forest and bluff echo the coughing of the high pressure steamboat, the Roarer; and now she passes the mouth of the sluggish Illinois, which glides into the Mississippi like an overgrown eel. Onward struggles the Roarer, puffing and wheezing, and trembling in every joint; the shores, dimly lighted by the blaze of the boat's furnaces, seem still as wide asunder as those of the lower Mississippi. On one shore rises an abrupt bluff to the height of forty or fifty feet, and the other is a bank of fresh crumbling alluvion, being the terminus of a wide plain which seems to be dissolving in the river. And now, as night advances, there is seen far up the river, a steamboat rushing with the stream. Her furnaces, like eye-balls, glare in the darkness—flames stream from her tall black flues— the waters foam around her — and as she rushes by the Roarer her name, "Ione," printed upon her wheel-house, is scarcely legible, so quickly does she pass.

In the cabin of the Roarer sat several persons, some of whom were playing a game of brag. Two of the players seem to be professional gamblers. They belonged nowhere in particular, but inhabited the river generally, from the Balize to St. Peters. Bright shone the chandeliers suspended above the tables; but the night was far advanced and many of the passengers—the careful country merchant —the English tourist—the old man on a visit to the South —and the young man seeking his fortunes in the West, one after another retired to rest. One of these gentlemen in black was engaged in an interesting game of cards with Jefferson Randolph Rutledge, Esq., whose father had commissioned him to invest fifteen thousand dollars in the purchase of negroes in the upper country. Mr. Rutledge had great confidence in his own ability—in his own ability to beat anybody in the world at a game of brag or at anything else. He is in bad luck that night, and has already lost thirteen thousand dollars. Mr. Black, who was pitted against him, played coolly. Believing that Rutledge's pile was nearly exhausted, he determined to overbrag the young gentleman, and oversize his pile. Rutledge held three "bullets" and bragged a thousand dollars.

"Two thousand better," says Black.

Rutledge looked dismayed—he was broke. A stranger standing at his elbow who had watched the game and saw that Rutledge held a sure hand, lent him a large bundle of bank notes, and whispering to him, "here, young man are fifty thousand dollars, brag it all." In the meantime Mr. Black had borrowed all the funds of his fellow blacklegs to meet the emergency.

"Fifty thousand better," says Mr. Rutledge.

"I am broke," replies Black, pushing his pile across the table to his adversary. "Here is only thirty thousand; for the remaining eleven thousand, sir, you must take an I O U;" and thus ended the game of "brag." The passengers slept; but the engine rested not—the fiery furnaces were unquenched, and the Roarer still dashed onward, and the watchful eye of the pilot in the wheel-house soon discovered another boat, the "Orion," coming in the rear of the Roarer. "Hurrah for a race!" shouts the mate. "Wood up! boys, wood up! They say this new low pressure boat, the Orion, outruns lightning." The Orion came darting along, without much apparent exertion; gaunt and slender as a greyhound. The firemen of the Roarer were splitting their wood fine; and having dipped it in barrels of tar, they plunged it into the furnaces. Columns of black smoke, commingled with the flame, poured from the flues. The firemen sweated and swore, and swilled whisky—the pulsations of the paddles were quickened to a fearful rapidity.

The Roarer trembled and struggled forward like a maniac. Her escape pipe whistled the shrill note of alarm, but it was smothered by adding weight to the safety-valve. Barrels of rosin were pitched into the furnaces, and lard and hams were sacrificed, but in vain; for the Orion slowly stole alongside, and the two rival boats ran side by side, neck by neck, for half an hour, until at length the Roarer fell gradually in the rear.

While the Orion was running alongside of her antagonist, a fine muscular young man, dressed in the uniform of Texas, leaped like a panther from the Roarer's guards onto the deck of the Orion. Having alighted, he turned to the captain of the Roarer, and told him very politely that he felt anxious to reach Galena, and hoped, therefore, the captain would excuse him for taking as speedy conveyance as possible. In two minutes after the Roarer was blown up. As the young man, whose name is White, is the hero of my tale, I will briefly inform the readers how he happened to be on board the Roarer.

It is sufficient for the present to say that he was on his return from Texas. Of course he was out of funds; for although it was very common for men to carry money into Texas, it was very uncommon for them to bring any away. The poor devil was completely broken down; and, to tell the truth, had not the means of paying his passage up the river. He had fought at the battle of San Jacinto—held a commission in the army of Texas—frequented the levees of Sam Houston—and danced fandangoes with the Spanish girls of Mexico. He had seen prosperity and adversity—had been in battle, and oftener in love; and, in short, although not twenty-five years of age, Jim White had seen all sorts of life.

CHAPTER II.

THE CITY OF GALENA AND THE MINERAL REGION.

If this biography should chance to be read by any reader living east of the Allegheny Mountains, that reader may be curious to know what, if not even where, the city of Galena is. On the evening of the 5th day of September at about sunset, the Orion turned her bow eastward into the channel of a sluggish little stream called Fevre River, and after winding her way between precipitous bluffs for half a dozen miles, she was moored in the city of Galena. The town is built in the amphitheatre of hills; and at first view appears like a flock of houses coming down to water. The river appears to have its source under the town. The buildings back of Main street rise one above the other like theatre boxes; and, in short, Galena, take it all in all, is one of the most grotesque little cities in the world. It has its mayor, aldermen and common council, its ordinances and police regulations like the cities on the Atlantic seaboard; and cuts a figure much like a boy who has just exchanged his frock for pantaloons and jacket. When the traveler beholds the large quantities of lead piled upon the levees and considers that Galena is the principal outlet for the richest and most extensive mineral regions in the world, he will no longer wonder "what the devil Galena is encamped there for!"

A few years ago, Galena was a mere hamlet containing a few miners' cabins and groceries, and a few courageous-hearted men, who did battle with Black Hawk and his warriors and drove them across the Mississippi. Since then the mines have been in the peaceable possession of the whites, and the manufacture of lead has gone on steadily increasing. New and valuable discoveries have been made every succeeding year; and the agricultural interest of the mining region has advanced hand in hand with the mining interests.

Mr. White went ashore (he had no baggage, not even a spare shirt, which candor alone compels the writer to acknowledge), and took lodgings in the " Northwestern Hotel." Having registered his name as " Major James White, of the army of Texas," he took a seat and made himself at home. The next morning he took up a newspaper called the *Galena Telescope and Sucker Times*, in which amongst other important items of intelligence he read the following:

"TERRIBLE STEAMBOAT EXPLOSION, ETC."

"The steamboat Roarer, on her passage up from St. Louis, when a little below Quincy, burst her boiler; by which means all the passengers, save the mate and one engineer were blown into eternity. Beans are rising in St. Louis, and large sales of lead were made on Monday at one-fourth per cent. advance on the prices on Saturday. The names of the passengers on the Roarer are unknown, and the causes of the explosion also; no blame is to be attached to the officers of the boat. The Orion was just ahead of her when she exploded; but not near enough to know of the disaster or to afford any relief. State Bank of Illinois remains in *statu quo*.

"P. S.—The Roarer was insured for thirty thousand dollars in St. Louis by the Rushlight Assurance Company, which company, upon the news of this disaster, will no doubt go into liquidation, as all the principal stockholders in that institution have taken the benefit of the bankrupt act, and the shares been transferred to assignees. The Washingtonians are carrying all before them. The large wholesale house of Fawcette, Spiggot, Decanter & Co., wine and spirit dealers, has made an assignment and gone into liquidation."

Mr. White lighted a cigar and walked out into the city to reconnoitre. He saw some fine houses, but they were not his ; and some large stores and warehouses, but he was none the better for them; and some elegant churches, in which perhaps the soul might feast, but which could furnish him nothing to satisfy his necessities. He looked at the desolate knobs and hills encamped around and saw the countless holes that had been dug by miners with various success, and seating himself alone upon a rock afar off upon the pinnacle of a hill that overlooked the town, he began to soliloquize: "Ten years ago I embarked in a skiff at Olean, and dropped down the Allegheny river to Pittsburgh and saw for the first time the magnificent Valley of the Mississippi spread out like a map before me. Then as my imagination swarmed with the creations of fancy, how little did I dream that in ten years I should be cast a penniless soldier upon the shores of the Mississippi to dig in the mines. Texas! why, the revolution of Texas was not then talked of, and here I am at the age of twenty-five a veteran of the revolutionary army of Texas. I wish Texas had been at the devil and I at my business making myself wealthy and respectable in some honest pursuit; but here I am a vagabond! I see that my military coat is getting out at the elbows. Well, the amount of the business is, I must dig."

The "lead district" is embraced in the original Northwest Territory, ceded to Congress by the State of Virginia. Upon the extinguishment of the Indian title, the fee simple of course vested in Congress. The upper lead district as it is generally called, extends about seventy miles north and south on both sides of the Mississippi river, and about sixty miles east and west, embracing portions of Iowa, Wisconsin and Illinois. Perhaps the most prominent feature in the face of the country, is the "Mounds." They are quite numerous; among the most prominent of which, are, the Blue

Mounds, the Sinsinnawa, and Platte Mounds—some of these mounds are one or two hundred feet high, and appear to be nothing more or less than hills dissolved by time, and by the gradual disintegration of the rocks of which they are composed; rugged mountains razed into smooth, green mounds. Standing upon one of these the traveler sees the mining region spread out before him like a map. The greater part of the land is prairie; though there is abundance of forest and barrens. The prairie is mostly undulating; but the forest and barrens are strongly marked with ridges and ravines. No country in the world is more abundantly watered. Every ravine has its rivulet. The most successful mining operations have been in the barrens, where the land is broken into irregular lobes or swells, ranging in altitude from ten feet to one hundred. In "prospecting," the miner generally commences by digging a hole as large as a well, on the north and south side of these hills, in some small ravine leading up the side. If, in sinking the shaft he finds scattered mineral—" float" as it is termed, he infers that it descended from an east and west crevice above. It is then termed a prospect, and the miner is encouraged to sink another hole a few feet further up the ravine. If in the next shaft he finds the mineral still "stronger," that is, larger, more abundant, and of a character indicating the near approach to the crevice from which it "floated," he throws into a pile all the pieces of mineral he has found and calls it a "show"—a good show or a bad show as the fact may be. The speculator, upon examination of a show, often buys the discoverer's show or prospect of a "lead." The mere prospect of finding a lare body of mineral is frequently sold for hundreds of dollars. The miner now proceeds to prove his "prospect;" that is to extend a range of prospect holes up the hill to the crevice. If he should pass over the crevice, in prospecting, he will find no mineral in the holes he may sink; because mineral never floats up hill. He then commences "drifting," that is, digging horizontally from the bottom of the last hole in which he "struck" mineral, towards the bottom of the next hole above, and in his progress he strikes the crevice, which may, after all the labor in finding it, be a barren crevice, containing but little mineral; on the other hand, the lead may be worth many thousands of dollars; since the labor of raising the mineral when discovered is comparatively little, and the ore is worth when raised from ten to twenty-five dollars per thousand pounds. "Crevices," of course vary in depth and width. Some of these are openings thirty or forty feet wide, between perpendicular wall rocks. The ore is generally found mixed with ochre and flint—but is sometimes found in solid masses.

When all the mineral is raised that can be found in sinking a shaft the miner commences drifting east and west in the crevice for more mineral. For this purpose it is sometimes necessary to brace the aperture with timbers to prevent caving. Sometimes a lead is worked out by means of a level; that is, a tunnel being dug in the bottom of the crevice through the hill, and in this tunnel is constructed a cheap railroad for carrying out the contents of the crevice. The principal crevices run east and west; those running north and south contain smaller quantities, generally in thin horizontal sheets, and are cut out by east and west leads (or as geologists term them "lodes"). Sometimes after drifting a few rods the crevice "closes up," but frequently by sinking another hole still further east or west on the same crevice, another "opening" is found, and the mineral comes in good again. Leads vary greatly in extent. Some are wide and deep, while others are narrow and shallow. Some "run" well, while others "give out" in a few rods. Occasionally a crevice is found widening into a "chamber" containing an immense body of mineral. It is not, however, every crevice that contains mineral—the sanguine miner sometimes comes to the bottom of a barren crevice, confident all the time that he is about to strike mineral; and when, after all his labor, he finds the crevice closed up at the bottom with solid rock, he leans perhaps on the handle of his pick, the very image of despair, and then ascends into the light of day by means of a 'windlass. In some places the diggers have run the mineral into the water. Of course these water leads cannot be worked unless by draining and pumping.

Some miners and geologists believe that much larger bodies of lead and also of copper ore, lie buried deep in these mines, than have yet been discovered. For mining deep, much capital and large and expensive machinery is requisite. The population of the mines is rather fluctuating, drifting from one part of the mines to another and settling permanently nowhere. This state of things is of course unfavorable to the steady growth and permanent prosperity of the towns and villages in the mines. All the lands in the "lead district" which were known by government to be mineral lands, and some which were not supposed to be mineral lands, but which were covered with forests to supply the wants of miners and smelters, have been reserved from sale "for mining and smelting purposes." Many tracts of land not reserved, have been entered, that is, purchased at the land office. Before entering a tract of land a purchaser was sometimes required to make oath that he knew of no mineral having been discovered upon it. If the miner discovers a valuable lead upon Congress land, and the discovery is known to no other person, the inducement to perjury by taking the oath required at the land office, and purchasing the soil in fee simple at one dollar and a quarter per acre, is great. Perhaps some frauds upon the Government have been thus committed. No patents for these lands have yet been issued; if such frauds have been committed, they may become the subject of legal investigation. Mineral lands thus purchased are of course leased by the proprietors upon such terms as they please to establish. A great part of the lands reserved from sale have, by a kind of prescription, become also the property of claimants in the following manner: They were at first farmed out to miners in small lots, by an agent of government. The miner was allowed to stake out his lot which he was then authorized by a "permit" from the agent to occupy, upon the condition of his mining upon the lot five days in every week, etc. Few, if any, of the miners complied with the condition of their permits; but the miners were indulgent toward one another, and each respected the claims of the rest; so that although the lots were forfeited, no complaint was made to the agent. Permits soon began to be transferred by sale, like leases; and every purchaser of a mineral lot held it by a title deemed even better than that by which the first claimant held; because a valuable consideration had been paid. The revenue for the mines was collected from the smelter, who purchased his ore from the miner. Each smelter received a license from the government, and was required to pay over to the agent one-tenth part of all the lead he manufactured. Thus the revenue was paid indirectly by the miner.

Many valuable leads were discovered upon lands which had been entered at the land office. The proprietors of such lots were of course under no obligations to pay rents to the government. They required the smelter to pay them the full value for their mineral. But the smelter was bound to pay over one-tenth part of the lead manufactured by him as revenue to the government, whether manufactured from ore raised upon "reserved" lands or "entered" lands. The smelter could not ascertain whether the mineral brought to him was raised on government land or not. If he had been allowed to attempt a discrimination, it would have been unavailing; since nothing could be easier than for a miner upon government land to sell his ore to a neighbor who owned a mineral lot in fee simple, and who would sell the ore as his own, without any deductions for rent. The revenues for rent naturally soon became nearly nominal. The smelters were environed with difficulties. In the year 1836, the whole system went down, every smelter refusing to pay rent. The agency ceased, and government was fairly "elbowed" out of the mining district. The possession of such reserved mineral grounds as had been claimed by miners under the old regulations by virtue of permits, was left undisturbed. The proprietors, as they consider themselves, lease these lands to miners upon such terms as they deem most profitable, some taking one-fourth, others one-fifth of the mineral raised. A great number of mineral lots are in many instances the property of the same landlord, some successful speculator in lead perhaps, who has bought up, at a bargain, the claims of many poorer men. Whether these tenures were exactly honest in their origin or republican in their tendency, will not here be made a subject of inquiry. No doubt the most profitable disposition Congress could make of their mineral lands would be to sell them in small lots to the highest bidders. By such sale a large sum of money would accrue to the treasury—as great, perhaps, in the aggregate, as the lands are intrinsically worth; and more profit would thus be derived from them than could be derived from the best system of renting and leasing that could be devised. The expense and endless perplexities arising from the establishment and support of agencies for leasing the lands and collecting the rents would thus be avoided, and Congress would be saved from the odium always in our country attached to the character of a landlord exacting his rents. The mineral resources of the lead district, or at least those which are accessible to the labor and industry of the small capitalists have been exaggerated. Most of the leads near the surface of the ground have been discovered. That there are large bodies of copper, as well as of lead ore, in these mines, buried deep in the bowels of the earth—such bodies of mineral as have been found in the Cornish mines—is quite possible, but the working of mines to any considerable depth requires the investment of large capital in machinery, etc., and is not likely to be undertaken until the mines become the exclusive property of those who have capital to invest in working them. If Congress, in its wisdom, should deem it inconsistent with the rights of the parties concerned, and the greatest good to the greatest number, to sell these mines to private purchasers, it might nevertheless be considered judicious to surrender them to the States in which they are, or the Territories when they shall become States, of which they shall form an integral portion, upon such conditions as may be just and equitable to the other States of the confederacy. It is certain that a State can manage revenues of this description better than Congress.

The business of smelting is quite distinct from that of mining. The smelter must have some capital to do business. He constructs a furnace, usually in a ravine near the diggings and over some small stream of water which is used as well for washing the mineral as for turning the water-wheel that works the furnace bellows. The process of smelting is simple enough. The mineral is broken fine and thrown into a large slanting hearth filled with charcoal and wood. When, by action of the bellows, the heat becomes sufficiently intense, the lead begins to trickle down the hearth in bright streams, which unite and flow through one mouth into a reservoir, which is also heated. From this reservoir the melted lead is removed with a ladle and poured into moulds made of cast-iron. When thus moulded into "pigs," weighing about seventy pounds each, the lead is ready for the market. The per centum yielded by good mineral is about seventy or eighty. The ore contains a small quantity of silver; though perhaps too little to warrant the cost of extracting it; the residuum is called "slag."

CHAPTER III.

A SCENE IN THE MINES.

Jim White remained in Galena one month. His landlord began to treat him cavalierly; for, with the unerring instinct of a publican, he had guessed the true state of Mr. White's finances.

"Mr. White," quoth he, as Jim was exchanging his slippers for boots one morning. "Mr. White, I have a trifling bill of twenty dollars for four weeks' board, which I will trouble you to cash."

"No doubt," coolly replied Mr. White; "but such is the state of my finances—"

"You poor, trifling rascal," interrupted the landlord— "You poor, trifling vagabond, sir, leave my house sir!"

"Certainly, sir," says White, "I leave your house in disgust. You are quite undeserving the patronage of gentlemen. —— you and your house, too!"

Blue Rabbit diggings, on little Blue Rabbit Creek, is in the Territory of Wisconsin, and is distant from Galena three hours' ride. The hamlet consists of fifteen or twenty miners' cabins, straggling carelessly along the creek, like Irish shanties; moreover there were three groceries, connected with one of which there was a ninepin alley, or "horse billiard room," where the clatter of falling pins and the rumbling of the balls could be heard twenty-four hours in each day and seven days in each week; for Sunday, with its sober quiet, was a stranger in these "diggings," and prayers were as uncommon as earthquakes. Since then the temperance reform, which swept lately like a hurricane through the Valley of the Mississippi, has scattered to the four winds of heaven the last vestige of a grog-shop in Little Blue Rabbit, but, at the period of time of which I am writing, the ball alley grocery was thronged. Some were playing cards, some were smoking, some laughing, and others swearing; and no scene could be found richer in degradation and vice in the most degraded basement of the "Five Points."

"Set up the pins there, boy! Stand away from the ball!" shouted a six-footer, dressed in a buffalo robe.

Away rolled the ball.

"Good luck," quoth little weazel-faced John Smith.

The second ball swept down the remaining pins

"Spare ball, by ——!" shouted all.

Rice Hawkins, a black-haired, billious looking rascal, with a deep sunken eye in his head, whose mate he had left in Kentucky, rolled next. His first ball struck down only the centre pin,

"Perfect gut!" says Buff.

The second ball ran into the trough, and the third ball struck the pin that was prostrate and bounded over against the bull's hide.

Hawkins poured out a broadside of chain-shot curses, as if he were a living magazine of blasphemy.

The last roller took the alley. He was twenty-five years of age, five feet ten inches in height. His countenance was open and expressive—his head, of the best phrenological model, covered with light brown hair—a scar on his forehead, and his eye full of language. He wore a blue military frock coat, out at the elbows, drab pants buttoned up to the knees outside and a checquered shirt, which appeared as if it were destitute of a comrade to relieve it from duty.

"Roll away, stranger!" said little Smith.

"My name," replied the person addressed, coolly selecting his balls, "is Jim White—at your service."

White rolled with great precision. His first ball struck the head pin a little quartering so as to sweep the alley.

"Ten strike!" roared the company.

White took the pool, paid for the alley and treated all hands. The noise, and babbling and boasting increased and soon reached the fighting point.

"Who dar say," roared Buff, smiting his fists together, "that I am not the best man in the house? or in Blue Rabbit? or in the mines?"

"Did you ever fight an alligator in the Okefenokee swamp?" retorted Mr. White.

"You take it up!" roared Bluff. "You take it up? You blue-bellied gallinipper! I'll *hoop* you to death in a minute!"

Upon this the fight commenced. Both combatants were armed. White instantly drew a large bowie knife from a pocket or sheath on the back side of his neck. His adversary drew a similar weapon from the skirt of his coat-pocket. They glared at each other for a moment. White received a cut on the left arm, and instantly aimed a blow at Buff's heart, by which the breast of his coat was torn open and a flesh wound inflicted.

Knives and pistols leaped from their scabbards, and the row became general. However, as nobody was killed or much hurt, the whole affair was forgotten in a few minutes or remembered only as an agreeable little pastime of almost daily occurrence.

"Give us your hand, comrade," said Jim, helping his adversary up. "I don't want to hurt you; but ——— ———

my roaring soul if any man must say he is a *better* man than Jim White. Ho! landlord! liquor for the crowd."

The barkeeper placed sixteen tumblers on the counter. Some took cogniac, others monongahela, while others chose gin—rum—'alf and 'alf, etc., all of St. Louis manufacture.

"Walk up, gentlemen, and help yourselves, the liquor is free. Old Buff, here's to your better luck!"

"Good hand," replies Buff; "fire up down below."

It is now midnight—and we leave this crowd to find lodgings for the night the best way they can; heartily hoping that they will go home, and "never get drunk any more."

PROSPECTING.

One frosty morning in October, as the smoke was streaming up in plumes from the chimney of every shanty in Blue Rabbit diggings, you might have seen, had you been there, a man dressed in an old blue military frock coat and drab pantaloons, at work in a small mineral hole which was being sunk in a small ravine extending at right angles up the bluff from the principal ravine in a southerly direction. Several fresh holes had been dug north of that over which the windlass stood. By the side of the windlass was a hat, and hanging on a bush nearby was a large buffalo coat with a hole five or six inches long slit in the breast of it. The man at the windlass wound up the rope at the end of which was a tub filled with reddish clay. The tub appeared to be the half of a barrel sawed in two, with a rope bail. The man at the windlass, Major James White, late of the army of Texas, then seized the tub by the bail, swung it onto the platform with his left hand, disengaged the wooden hook from the bail and emptied the tub. It was hard work; but still the Major looked as contented as a badger "to the manner born." Gentle reader, if you are tormented with blue devils, or distressed with *ennui*, or lack an appetite for food or the means of gratifying it—if you are out of spirits, out of funds, out of patience, out of picayunes, out at elbows and tempted to get out of the world, go and tend windlass for a week.

"Hook!" roared a voice from the hole.

The hook without the tub was instantly lowered down and almost as quickly drawn up again. The proprietor of the buffalo coat came rising out of the hole, pale as a spectre, and trembling violently. Jim White seized Buff by the arm, pulled him onto the platform, his foot still hanging in the hook, and laid him on the ground. Jim then brought some water in a jug from Little Blue Rabbit Creek near by, and soon restored his partner. How inconsistent is man! To-day he aims his murderous steel at the heart of his fellow and to-morrow, perchance, risks even his own life to save the same individual from danger.

"Is it the damps, partner?" inquired Jim kindly, at the same time bringing Buff's coat to him, which he had so lately slashed with a bowie knife.

"Yes—the damps," answered Buff.

"How do the damps seem at first to affect one?" quoth Jim.

"Why," replies Buff, "when you have been in the damps awhile, breathing don't do you any good. It's just like breathing nothing, you understand. You just naturally grow dizzy and faint away."

"Well," quoth Jim, "what is the damps anyhow? Give me the philosophy of the thing?"

"The *feel*-o-sophy, Jim? Is it how you feels you want to know?" says Buff.

"No, no," quoth Jim, laughing; "I only meant to inquire what the damp is."

"Oh," said Buff, "I suppose it is just solid air, so thick that you can't breathe it."

CHAPTER IV.

THE MINER'S CABIN.

The next morning at sunrise Jim was getting breakfast for himself and partner at the shanty where they "bachelored." Buff had not yet risen from his bunk on the back side of the shanty. Jim White seemed to be cooking very scientifically over a fire built in the bottom of a large stone chimney, which served as the only window when the door was shut. In the hot ashes were buried some potatoes. Two large slices of ham were frying in a two-legged spider; a coffee pot stood glowing upon the coals in the opposite corner of the fireplace. In one end of the shanty was a pile of potatoes upon the ground, and over the pile of potatoes were hanging a ham, a shoulder of pork and a saddle of venison. The table was such an one as might be made in ten minutes with an ax and auger, being simply an oaken board with four oaken legs inserted in as many auger holes.

There is no time when thought bubbles up in the mind as after a refreshing sleep.

"Ha! ha! ha!" laughed Buff, rising.

"Why, what are you laughing at, Buff?" inquired Jim.

"Why," says Buff, "when I saw you trying to get breakfast in the awkward way that men always do, I could not help thinking what an excellent invention a woman is! A thought has struck me."

"The devil there has, Buff! Why I should as soon expect the lightning to strike you," quoth Jim.

"I will tell you," says Buff, "I have an idea—"

"Oh," interrupted Jim, "if you have only *one* idea do keep it for *seed*."

"No, I have laid a plan," quoth Buff, "which I will unfold to you."

"Ah!" inquired Jim, "that reminds me that I have something *to unfold to you.* Here is a bill of items which I found stuck under the door this morning and addressed to you. It is an interesting document—I have had many similar favors in my day and may look for more unless I take the benefit."

"Pray read it to me," quoth Buff, "for I am no scholar. I had too much important business on hand when I was a boy, to learn to read and write."

"Certainly," replied Jim, "I will read it."

	Mr. Buff—	
184—	To Nero E. Gripe,	Dr.
June 10,	To one buffalo coat	$18.00
" 15,	To 30 lbs. windlass rope at 31c	9.31
July 9,	To 1 pair buckskin pants	7.00
" 30,	To 1 round-topped miner's hat	1.50
Aug. 15,	To 1 pick	2.00
Sept. 12,	To tobacco, pipes and sundries	13.00
	Total	$50.81

Mr. Buff—Please call and settle the above bill in cash or mineral and save cost. NERO F. GRIPE.
Per Joel Jackal, Clerk.

"Whew!" quoth Buff, "old Gripe be——! Thirteen dollars for sundries, ha! that must mean armbarillas, ha? Why I never bought an armbarilla in my life."

"No, no," says Jim, laughing, "sundries in this bill means whisky."

"Very good, then," quoth Buff, "it is all perfectly right. I will never refuse to pay for necessaries when I have mineral."

THE MINER'S CAMP. 27

"Well, Buff," says Jim, "the potatoes are done, and we will breakfast in spite of old Gripe. Stuff the devil when thou canst, as old King Nehemiah says in his book of proverbs. Let those borrow trouble who have money to lend. Now, Buff, unfold to me the plan you say you have laid."

"Why, then, you must know," says Buff, "that I am getting tired of digging for unsartainties; just as though there were not unsartainties enough atween heaven and airth, without probing the airth for more of 'em. The fact is, thar is a great deal more dirt in the ground than mineral."

"Astonishing!" exclaimed Jim, "what a discovery!"

"Besides," said Buff, "I want the privilege of breathing while I live. Now, I hold and am always ready to maintain, that it is just as natural for a man to breathe as to drink whisky. Therefore, a man *in* the damps is as unhappy as a fish *out* of water."

"What is that you are saying, partner?" quoth Jim, "not dig? And as pretty a crevice as we are in—mineral going down—pretty joint clay—and mineral ashes running down in an east and west crevice between regular wall rocks? Not dig? Why, the man is crazy! Let me tell you we have a pretty show. Not dig!"

"Land me in heaven," replies Buff, "if I dig to-day. True, Jim, we have a fine show. Two years ago our prospect might have sold for a thousand dollars. With good management it may be sold now. We need the ready. I am an old miner, Jim; I came to the diggings before the *Sauk furse*—saw the first steamboat that disturbed the waters of Fevre River, 'the Old Virginia.' I have struck a power of mineral in my day—good shows and not so good —fine prospects and not so fine. Jim, there are tricks in all trades. We have a sure thing when we get it; but I know by the float we are on that the main body of mineral lies east of us in the bowels of the hill. We might sell our prospect to a fool and strike it big afterwards. The ground we are on won't bear mineral—it won't run—but on yon swell to the east it is stronger."

"Why not dig there then at once," inquired Jim.

"Bekase," quoth Buff, "it might peter out, and if so be we should strike nothing, how could we sell out?"

"Exactly," says Jim, "I begin to comprehend your meaning. You go on the principle that a bird in hand is worth two in the bush. You would sell our prospect for a certain sum and run the risk of making a lead of it when the buyer has abandoned it?"

"With your consent, then, we will dress up our prospect for sale," replied Buff.

"Dress it!" replies Jim, "What do you mean by dressing it? We have nothing even to dress ourselves, but rags."

"Ha! ha! haw! haw! well, well," quoth Buff, "have you never hearn tell of grafting a mineral hole? Graft the hole; graft the hole, boy. Why, you must be soft. We have mineral enough to dress up a prospect hole beautifully. This is what I call dressing up a prospect for sale."

"That would be wrong," replies Jim.

"No," rejoined Buff, taking a chew of cavendish, "no, I will prove that it is perfectly right according to the established usages of the world. Does not all mankind put the best foot foremost? Does not the merchant put up show boxes to attract customers? Do not good men put on airs to make themselves pass in better company? What is a fashionable lady but a show dressed up to cheat some poor devil in a matrimonial bargain? In short, this world is all a fleeting show."

"But who would buy?" says Jim.

"Oh, leave that to me," quoth Buff, with an air of authority, "do you suppose the fools are all dead?"

A GREAT MAN IN GALENA.

Wealth is power, and Americans with all their democracy bow the knee to Mammon. No sooner is it reported that the wealthy Mr. Leech and his beautiful lady have arrived in Galena, and taken lodgings at the North Western Hotel, than the whole town is filled with gossip and anxiety to see the distinguished strangers. And pray who was Mr. Leech, that all this fuss and prattle should be made about him?

Was he a man of as much real worth, integrity, or talent as Jim White, who had lately been denied the hospitality of the North Western Hotel, and been spurned from it with contempt because he was too poor to pay for a month's board? Not half. The difference was this: Jim White had robbed and beggared himself, and was despised; Leech had robbed and beggared others, and was honored. He was the ex-cashier of the Mulberry & Baden Corn Banking Company of Wildcat, Feline County, Michigan; from whence he had just arrived with one hundred thousand dollars, being all the cash funds of the bank, and to which he had no right but that of possession. Mr. Funk, the landlord, was all attention; the lackeys were all obsequiousness, and all Galena was ransacked to furnish the table of the illustrious Mr. Leech with dainties. Mr. Funk ordered three baskets of champagne, three dozen of Madeira, three boxes of fruit, three dozen of poultry, and other table luxuries in proportion; so that the retail business of Galena flared up as it was wont to do in other days under the influence of bank expansions.

CHAPTER V.

GRAFTING A MINERAL HOLE.

Buff was as prompt to execute as he was shrewd to plan. The next morning at sunrise he and his partner had conveyed all their mineral to the last prospect hole they had sunk. They then proceeded to "graft." Buff went to the bottom of the hole, and there embedded several large pieces of mineral.

He then inserted smaller pieces from the bottom of the hole to the top, on each side thereof, sticking them in thick all the way, and finishing the work as well as nature herself could have done it. The hole was completely gemmed and studded with sparkling ore, and presented every appearance of a rich and extensive lead, with large mineral still going down. It was a labor that occupied them nearly all day; and when completed, would have deceived the old scratch himself.

"*Ars celar artem!*" muttered White, looking with amazement at the ingenious fraud; "surely Buff you were born for a poet."

"Don't talk Indian to me," quoth Buff; do you suppose bekase I was out in the Saux fuss that I understand all the Indian tongues from Choctaw to Pottowatamie? if you have any fault to find, speak it out."

"*Ars celar artem* is Latin," rejoined Jim, "not Indian. It is a quotation from Horace; meaning the art to conceal art."

"Horace be d——," replies Buff; "Horace may be a good miner, but I can beat him to death at grafting a mineral hole. Art? there's no art about it; you only just make it look sort of naytural like."

By the next morning it began to be whispered about that Buff and Jim White had struck a lead. Three smelters had been to them by ten o'clock in the morning, to engage their mineral, and amongst them old Nero E. Gripe, who told Buff in a very bland conciliatory tone, that he would be happy to pay him cash for their mineral at his furnace; that he, Buff, had been an old customer at his store, and a good one; that he regretted to learn that Jackal, his clerk, had sent Mr. Buff a dunning letter a day or two previous. Mr. Jackal had certainly acted without the slighest authority from *him* in the matter, etc. Every grocery keeper in Blue Rabbit diggings insisted upon treating *Mr.* Buff and *Mr.* White; and Mr. Slop, the new merchant tailor, actually dragged them both into his store, and sent them away each in a new suit of clothes from head to foot.

"Did you say you were going into town to-day, Mr. Buff?" quoth Slop.

"Yes."

"Well now you want an overcoat; just try this on; it will fit you like an India rubber over-shoe. I can sell you this coat *cheaper* than you can buy it in Galena. Only twenty-four dollars! Will you have it?"

"Yes, I may as well," replied Buff; and back went the two partners to their humble cabin

"Now," says Buff, "I will tell you what must be done, Jim. You must go and take the rope from the windlass and keep these prying rascals from going down into the hole; and buy goods of every man in town on the strength of our "lead;" and by this means get them all interested in our

GRAFTING A MINERAL HOLE. 33

effecting a good *sale*, so that we may have the means of paying them. In the meantime, I will go to Galena and stop with your old landlord, Mr. Funk, to whom you owe twenty dollars for board, and get him interested in your behalf, for the sake of getting his pay, to find a customer amongst the adventurers in Galena; some gudgeon who will bite a well-baited hook, to come out and purchase our lead of you. Of course you will affect the *greenhorn*. I will send a man out, you may depend. Ask him ten thousand dollars, and take, in cash, what you can get. If I should come out *with* him, treat me as an hired servant of yours. You take?"

The evening of the same day found Buff enjoying his supper at Mr. Funk's hotel in Galena. Amongst the strangers there, was Mr. Leech, ex-cashier of the Mulberry & Baden Corn Banking Company, who had just absquatulated from Michigan with one hundred thousand dollars to which he had no title but possession. Through the dress and genteel disguise of this upper crust rascal, Buff seemed at once to look, as if by instinct.

"Mr. Buff," quoth Funk, "I think you said you were from Blue Rabbit Diggings, in the Territory?"

"Yes; I hail from there."

"How is mining? Raising much mineral out there?"

"Why no, landlord, I can't say as they are. Though luck comes in streaks, as it always did. Now, I've been digging nine years, and am poor yet; though in fact I once struck a nine thousand dollar lead, which, like a fool, I sold for five hundred; but luck is everything. There came a poor devil of a greenhorn into our diggings a few weeks ago, who couldn't tell dry-bone from mineral—and he just dropped right down on the boomingest *kind* of a lead."

"Is it possible?" quoth Mr. Leech. "What might it be worth? Would he sell out?"

"There is great uncertainty," says Funk, "about the value of these leads. It may be a mere *show* and worth nothing."

"*No show* about White's lead, I assure you gentlemen; I am an old miner, and pronounce it certain for a million and a half of mineral."

"Did you say White?" asked Funk eagerly, "Jim White."

"Yes," says Buff, coolly.

"Oh! ah!" exclaimed Funk, "then you have seen the lead. Of course, being an old miner, you can tell very nearly from its appearance, and from the way mineral runs in those diggings, about it."

"Yes; I ought to know something about it," replies Buff; "for I was at work when he struck it, and *might* have been a partner with him."

"Mr. Buff," whispered Leech, "I should like a few moments' private conversation with you. Bar-keeper, send a decanter and glasses to my room." These two honest gentlemen, being seated together in Leech's room, the dialogue proceeded as follows:

"No doubt, Mr. Buff, you feel chagrined at the reflection that you have no interest in White's lead; being at work for him at the time, and he probably owing his discovery more to your skill in mining than to anything else. Now suppose, for a reasonable compensation, that you go out with me to what-do-ye-call it diggings, and without any seeming concert with me, act as my factor in the purchase of this land?"

"Stranger!" replied Buff, with a look of virtuous indignation, "stranger! I am only a poor digger, but have always had the name of acting honestly. Do you think it would be right for me to help you defraud this poor greenhorn!"

"Keep cool! keep cool! Mr. Buff; reflect on what I have proposed. One hundred dollars does not grow on every bush. Are not leads often bought and sold? Every man makes the best bargain he can for himself. I ask you simply to act as my factor in this business transaction."

"When will you go?" says Buff, slowly pocketing two fifty-dollar bills which Leech offered him.

"*Immediately!* Mr. Buff. My wife is here. As soon as I can make arrangements for her to go Badgerton to-morrow morning in the stage, on a visit to her sister there, I will be ready to leave. Get you ready immediately."

SELLING A PROSPECT.

Starlight was fading away in the rosy dawn of day, when Leech and Buff rode together in the quiet hamlet of Blue Rabbit Diggings, and not a sound was heard but the ripple of the Little Blue Rabbit creek, as it stole down the crooked ravine, shining like silver thread in the pale light of the fading moon. Not a cur barked—not a chimney smoked; and the ex-cashier, as he stood shivering in the miner's cabin-door, thought of the warm parlor he had left in Michigan.

"Hallo! Jim; I have brought a stranger with me; a gentleman who is an agent of the government living at Prairie du Chien, and who lost his way."

"Invite him in, Mr. Buff," replies Jim, getting up. "Strangers are ever welcome at my poor cabin. Please start a fire, Mr. Buff."

"Mr. White, inquired Buff, "have you raised any mineral since I left?"

"No, I have been beset all the time by strangers from abroad, who are trying to buy my lead. Buff, I was strongly tempted to sell out to-day."

"What were you offered, Mr. White?"

"Mr. Stokes says he will pay me ten thousand five hundred dollars, if I will wait three days for him to raise the money."

During this dialogue, the parties all assembled around the kindling fire.

"Gentlemen," says Leech, "I have some curiosity to see this lead you speak of, and will call again after breakfast. Mr. Buff, be so good as to show me the tavern."

Buff directed him to the tavern, winking at him as they parted, as if to say, I'll attend to White's case, while you are absent.

"Honor among thieves!" said Buff, giving him one of his fifty dollar bills. "This d—— land shark has run away from one of the banks down east with *bags* of money—defalcated, as they call it when a man with ruffle shirt and silk gloves on, *steals.* He paid me a hundred dollars to help to cheat you out of the lead. Now play your part well, and stick for nine thousand dollars."

After breakfast, the three gentlemen walked together to the mineral hole.

"Jim," says Buff, "you think more of your mineral hole than I do. Now, if this gentleman makes you a liberal offer, you had better sell."

"I do not know as I want to *buy*," said Leech, affecting carelessness, "You have been offered a great price for your lead."

SELLING A PROSPECT. 37

"I consider," added Buff, "that you ought to remember, Jim, when you have money offered you, that you are owing *me* something, and I want my *pay;* I need it, and can't well wait for you to speculate."

"Don't get uneasy, Mr. Buff, about your wages. I shall probably raise mineral enough to pay you off, Mr. Buff. You would not have asked me for your wages, Mr. Buff, if I had not struck this lead."

"*You* struck the lead, Jim? Yes, with my help! and it would only be liberal in you to make me a handsome present.

"I *will* be liberal with you Buff; never you mind. But now tell me candidly, Buff, as you are an old miner, would you take fifteen thousand dollars for the lead?"

"Jim, you know I am a friend of yours; but I scorn to meddle with other men's bargains; I *will* say, though, Jim, that I would take a *great deal* less. But every man for himself. There is not over thirty thousand to the foot."

Leech came up from the mineral hole with eyes as big as pealed onions.

"Well Mr. White, what is the least you will sell for?" says Leech, pale with excitement.

"Ten thousand dollars," replied Jim, the words faltering on his lips.

"I will give you nine, Mr. White."

"I will take it, Mr. Leceh. The lead is yours."

"Mr. Buff," quoth Leech, paying White a thousand dollar check on the Suffolk Bank of Boston, "Mr. Buff, please witness that I pay Mr. White one thousand dollars, to bind this bargain."

The parties went to a magistrate, and in one hour the conveyance was made—the remaining eight thousand dollars paid—and Mr. Leech became proprietor of a *grafted mineral hole.*

JUMPING A LEAD.

On the day Buff went to Galena, little weazel-faced John Smith and one-eyed Bill Hawkins met together at the grocery where we first found them, when the following dialogue ensued between them:

"I say, Bill, how the devil comes it that Buff and Jim White should pop down on such a heap of mineral?"

"Why, John, you know the old proverb, 'Poor men for children and fools for luck.' It isn't because they are any *peerter* than we, I reckon there's a heap of smarter men."

"Bill, I've a notion that they are about on a range with our old diggings, east. You know we found good mineral going down amongst the tumbling rock in all them are holes we sunk. Let us go and take a look."

"N. C., John; that is 'nuff said; keep dark."

In an hour after this, Mr. Smith and Hawkins were sinking a shaft under their windlass, about fifty rods due east of Buff and White's shaft on the same range and lot; and they *did* keep dark; for only two or three persons knew they were digging there for some days. They commenced digging there on the 21st day of October.

CHAPTER VI.

DIVIDING THE SPOILS.

" Buff!"

" Jim!"

" Well!"

" Well, back again and see how you like that. Ha! ha! Whoo! whoop! hurra! I *will* yell. Hold me Jim, nine thousand dollars, by the horned spoon! Clar the kitchen! Come, divide the spoils, Jim."

" To be sure Buff; honor bright! And as you are a Benton man, you shall have two hundred half eagles in your share; and here is the remaining three thousand five hundred dollars in treasury notes, said Jim, spreading the money upon the table before described. As for my share, Buff, I will take anything that will buy me pleasure. I intend to *spend* my money. Devil catch me, but I will live *broad*, if not quite as *long* as some. Who is it that compares money to a root? The Lord send me plenty of such roots while I live. I would feed no more on potatoes.

" Why, Jim, you talk as wild as a loon. What would you do, if you had as much money as that old Astor I hearn tell about, away down east, in New York, amongst the blue-bellied Yankees?"

" Do? Why, I would clear away all the buildings between the Battery and the Park, to build me a good, respectable dwelling house on, fit up the Astor House for my stable, and make a dog-kennel of the City Hall! I would be Nabob General of all North America."

"Keep cool! keep cool, Jim; we have service on hand yet. Leech has returned to Galena, and he will be here in a day or two to raise mineral. Ha! ha! Well, now, betwixt you and me, Jim, I have an *idea* his lead won't *run* well. I suspicion as how we've got the advantage of him in the trade. Well, as soon as he comes to raising mineral, no doubt he will accuse us of *cheating* him. That is just the natur of man. Then next, you know, he will be sueing us for a conspiracy to rob him, and then hurrah boys for a lawsuit! Jim you must go to Badgerton and see a lawyer."

"See the devil, Buff."

"I tell you, Jim, you must go and take counsel."

"Take *physic*, Buff."

"Well, Jim, call it physic if you like, but you *must* take it."

"Is it 'root hog or die,' Buff?"

"Them's 'em, exactly. To be sure, by running away you might save feeing a lawyer, and then again you moughtn't. No man who defends himself can be locked up with four thousand dollars in his pocket—it don't stand to reason. It is only those *poor devils* who has rent furnished 'em gratis at Doncaster. Wouldn't you scorn to have the county pay your house rent? Go to a lawyer—go to a lawyer, man. You must fight fire with fire; that is the way. A lawyer is as necessary as a boot-jack or windlass. Lawing without a lawyer, Jim, would be like mining without a pick. There is one lawyer there who will be sure to pick you up—fee him well. Ten to one Leech will go to him afterwards, and then we are safe."

"Won't he take a fee on both sides?"

"He daren't, Jim."

TAKING COUNSEL

The profession of law in the West is not generally the most lucrative business in the world. Many lawyers of much ability, in the mines, have been compelled, from time to time, to lay aside Blackstone and Chitty, and practice with the miner's spade and pick to make a living. Then again, it is generally supposed that three months spent in reading Blackstone and the statutes qualifies any man who has volubility of tongue and impudence of face, to practice law, and explain and unravel all the intricacies and subtleties of a science which, from its nature, is enlarged and extended by every additional volume of law reports; and the very elements of which might still be profitably studied by any lawyer during a lifetime as long as Methuselah's. Hence it happens that much of the law business that is to be done falls into the hands of impudent quacks, who, for half price half undo half the people who employ them, and thus bring the profession into contempt. It is due to the Badgerton bar to say, however, that its members are quite respectable.

"Walk in, sir," quoth Counsellor Power, rising, bowing several times very politely, and placing a chair for Mr. White; "very happy to make your acquaintance, Mr. White—sorry you find my office in such confusion, sir—please be seated, sir."

Upon this, the learned counsellor himself took a chair, tilted back in it and brushed his hair back with his right hand, just as my lord Chancellor might have done.

"I was just drafting a bill in chancery, Mr. White, for a young lawyer in the pinery, in *relation* to certain Indian Reservations; but will be happy to lay it aside, and attend to your business, sir."

"Why, I wish for your counsel, Mr. Power, in regard to a—to—that is—or, rather, I will state the case to you. I sold out my lead in Blue Rabbit Diggings to one Leech, for nine thousand dollars"—

"In cash?" asked Power.

"Yes, sir, in cash. Now, if he should be dissatisfied with his bargain, can he come back on me for damages?"

"Why, that will depend on circumstances, Mr. White. Did he buy on your representation, or did he go and look at the lead and examine it for himself?"

"He came, sir, and looked at it himself, and went down into the mineral hole."

"Well, sir, 'his eyes was his chap,' then; he can't hurt you for taking his money, when he bought entirely on his own judgment. Does he threaten to proceed?"

"Why, yes—that is, no—he don't exactly—exactly threaten; still, from what I have seen of the man, I should not wonder if he did."

"I understand, Mr. White. You wish to be prepared for him; an excellent idea, upon my honor. Ha! ha!

Quoth White, "If Leech should come to town for advice"—

"Exactly, exactly," responded Power. "I understand Mr. White. I will attend to that, you may depend."

"How much will be your fee, Mr. Power?"

"Why—ahem!—ha!—let me see—about—yes—this is a matter of considerable importance, Mr. White—about—oh! say a matter of fifty dollars."

"Here is your money, sir. Good day, Mr. Power."

"Good day! good day to you, Mr. White, and a pleasant ride. Call again, sir, do."

CHAPTER VII.

CAUGHT IN A GULL TRAP.

Mr. Leech returned from Blue Rabbit Diggings to Galena in high spirits, and splendid were the air-castles he constructed as he rode into the busy little city, and looked down, as from the gallery of a theatre, upon the bustle and activity in the streets; the loading and unloading of merchandise; the large quantities of bar lead, some of it in piles and some of it laid up in the manner of cob houses, upon the bank of Fevre River, awaiting the arrival of steamboats to transport it down the Mississippi River.

"Here," thought he, "will surely be a large city. It is on a fine navigable little river, only seven miles from the Mississippi, and in the heart of the mining country. This is the mart to which is brought all the lead manufactured by thousands of miners and smelters; here they sell their lead, always for cash; and here are purchased most of the goods and even provisions used in the mines. I will yet be an extensive lead merchant here, build me a good steamboat for the lead trade, erect a hotel like the Planter's in St. Louis, that will be fit for gentlemen who visit Galena to resort to; and on one side of this amphitheatre of hills I will cause to be built an elegant mansion for my private dwelling house. Let me see, there is a pretty site for my house on the hill back of the Catholic church. Ah! but won't I show these Galenians a pretty specimen or two in architecture? They do these things up better in Detroit. After all, what can be done without banks? Banking facilities—banking facilities—is what they want here. Trade needs a stimulus. There is no more stimulus in specie than there is in cold water. Would I not make a very respectable president of a bank? Let me think—yes, President of the—I have it now—the Blue Bullion Bank of Galena. Ha! ha! but didn't I play the devil at banking in Michigan? Well, let them come after me if they please; they can do nothing with me! Unfortunate—failed—ruined by speculation—a victim to the pressure of the times—all the fault of Old Hickory removing the deposits—and so on. After all, what is defalcation now-a-days? I foresaw embarrassment and saved myself the best way I could. Should I be an infidel and not provide for my own household? Everybody was preparing to make a run on the bank. I was bound to save myself the best way I could. Should I have let the vaults be robbed by the ragged rabble? Very clear of it. No, no. The world owes me a living, and I cheerfully place this hundred thousand to its credit. If the world is my debtor, then, and I hold its funds, why should I give them up? Shall I ever have a better opportunity to collect what the world owes me? Never. Besides had I retired from Wildcat destitute, I should have had no means to go into business here—could have obtained no bank facilities—could never have liquidated my debts, if I had desired to do so—and, in a word, could never have become the proprietor of this lead of mineral, by the purchase of which I have this day, I believe, made my eternal fortune."

The ex-cashier's reverie was here interrupted by his horse stopping at the stable door of Mr. Funk's Hotel, which stable too nearly resembles the house to deserve description. It being now generally understood about Galena that Mr. Leech had a large sum of money to invest in speculation and otherwise, that gentleman was hourly thronged with the company of persons anxiously solicitous to give him information how he could best dispose of his funds. One wanted to hire a few thousand dollars upon a mortgage of lots in Bellview, another had a span of beautiful dapple gray horses and a carriage, which he would sell at an immense sacrifice. Messrs. Shark & Co., knowing of his mineral purchase at Little Blue Rabbit, were desirous that he should contract to deliver them half a million of lead in Galena. Half a score of attorneys and as many doctors left their professional cards with him. In short, Mr. Leech was the lion of the day in Galena. Mr. Leech was too much a man of the world not to know the meaning of all these civilities; but who is secure amid a thousand gull-traps? The next day Mr. Leech was seduced into another mineral speculation. Mr. Jonas, a self-styled alchemist, with more brass in his face than silver in his pocket, called upon the ex-cashier and introduced himself as a gentleman who had lately discovered immense quantities of copper ore near Charleston, in the Territory of Iowa, about which so much had been said in the newspapers.

"It's a mint, Mr. Leech; a perfect mint, sir. Inexhaustible—quite inexhaustible. It is copper, sir—pure copper; virgin metal, sir, virgin. Look at these specimens, Mr. Leech. That copper is fit to coin sir—to coin. We only want capital to begin with—capital is all, sir," continued the alchemist with great enthusiasm. "I only want a gentleman of capital and intelligence—and intelligence, sir, to take an interest with me in the mine. We want money to erect buildings and machinery—machinery, you understand."

"But," interrupted Leech, "may you not over-estimate the value of this discovery, Mr. Jonas? How extensive is the mine, and has the quality of the ore been well tested?"

"Why, sir," replies Jonas, "as to the extent of the mine, it runs everywhere; there is any amount of it—any amount. The ore has been submitted to the examination of the best chemists in Cincinnati and New York, and they concur in pronouncing it the purest ever discovered. Ask anybody you please about Galena. Everybody has seen specimens—everybody." Here Mr. Jonas exhibited some fine specimens of copper ore, brought from Mineral Point, Wisconsin.

"I will show you a letter—a letter, sir, on the subject, which I have just received from New York."

Leech took the letter and read as follows:

NEW YORK, Aug. 18, 184—.

Mr. Jonas.

Sir—After making further and more careful analysis of the copper ore you sent us, we are confirmed in the opinion of its value we hastily formed and briefly expressed to you in our letter dated 1st of July last. We have to make you a conditional proposition for the purchase of an interest in your mine. Copper mining is not quite in our line of business, still we are Yankees enough to engage in lucrative speculation where we are confident of winning. Provided that we can be satisfied that the ore is generally as good as the specimens, and the mines as extensive as you represent, we will take one-fourth of it at twelve thousand five hundred dollars, and engage to find purchasers for the other three-fourths. Please consider our proposition and answer us immediately, and oblige

Your obedient servants,

BLOWPIPE & CRUCIBLE.

"Hum! ah! yes. Blowpipe? Blowpipe?" said Leech, musing and looking at the post mark. "So this is my old classmate! why, sir, I know Blowpipe well. He had always a great penchant for the laboratory; and used to get fuddled regularly every week by inhaling exhilarating gas. So, then, Blowpipe & Crucible"—

"Have taken a share—a share with me in the mine," interrupted Jonas. " But their payments are not due until half a million of ore is raised. I shall not ask them to advance one dollar, because they are not here to look at the purchase themselves. Now, can I enlist you in this enterprise? Take a share with me—take one-half and on your own terms—that is if you think well of the mine after seeing it."

"Why," replied Leech, "I think not—I rather think not, Mr. Jonas. I have just bought valuable lead diggings at Little Blue Rabbit, in Wisconsin, which I must work immediately. Where is your mine? Where is Charleston?"

"On the Iowa side of the Mississippi," answered Jonas. Only a few dozen miles below. The Otter is now getting up steam for St. Louis. Drop down with me to Charleston and see my mine, at least. We can return any day."

"Well, said Leech, "I should like the exercise at any rate, I will go. But do not rely upon selling to me. I don't know about these copper mines. I am afraid you are too sanguine?"

"The next day the elegant wife of the ex-cashier took stage for Badgerton. She was one of those few women whom every one inevitably loves. It was not altogether her beauty that made her attractive; it was more the winning smile—the elegant eye—but why attempt to tell what it was? One woman will be rather agreeable—another repulsive—and another fascinating. Mrs. L. was one of those women whom to see is to love. You could feel the tendrils of her heart entwining with yours. She seemed to have a natural affinity to man.

CHAPTER VIII.

MONEY MAKES THE MARE GO.

Major White now being in funds, suddenly became the lion of Badgerton. As if by magic, it was discovered that he was the best looking and the most accomplished man "of our acquaintance." Every lady in town sent her album to the Major, and every one was inquiring into the Major's history. It was generally reported that the Major had been an officer in the army of Texas, and, like most soldiers, had left the army with nothing except honor and glory, and that he had since become immensely rich in the mines. Miss Celia Persimmon, a young lady of twenty-five and upwards, who had refused three young men without leads, determined to win the Major. He had taken the best lodgings in town —sported the finest horse and buggy—wore the best clothes —smoked the best cigars—subscribed for the best periodicals, including the *Turf Register*—and was altogether a tip top fellow.

Unfortunately, the lady of the ex-cashier occupied apartments in a house exactly opposite the Major's rooms; so that the two respective occupants seemed destined to discourse together, at least in the language of the eyes.

Let a young man have nothing else to do, and of course, as he *must* do something, he will get in love; and why should a young lady be wiser? Dr. Watts says, that

> Satan finds some mischief still
> For idle hands to do.

Still, as there are counts enough in the indictment against his Satanic highness, I am not inclined to add this

charge to the number; and will therefore let the old fellow
off; although the introduction of a little infernal machinery
might add vastly to the epic grandeur and dramatic effect of
my story.

Day after day was the Major's attention directed across
the street, and riveted upon the beautiful woman who sat
looking out of the window opposite. He watched the rapid
changes that stole over her countenance. At one moment
she seemed gay, and her eyes laughed; at other times
she sat with her chin pensively resting upon her jeweled
hand, as calm as marble. She did not seem to observe the
Major. He had abandoned books, horses and everything
else in blind idolatry to this beautiful being, to whom he
had never yet so much as spoken. She became the very
light of his existence. He would have sacrificed all he possessed to win from her one look—one smile. He knew not,
cared not, who she was; he only knew that he loved her as
he had never loved woman before. Was she ignorant of
his sensations? By no means. There is a language—a
natural language—that betrays these secrets—that speaks in
every motion—in the countenance—and above all, in the
eye. She did not seem to see the Major—that meant something—it was *studied*. She had a perfect right to be looking out of the window; nor was she under the slightest ob-
ligation to see the Major. Again and again, a thousand
times each day, he looked. Every hour she seemed more
beautiful—more captivating. He felt that she must indeed
be capable of intense love. She was tall and graceful, and
twenty-five years of age; yet she looked much younger.
With a sigh of despair, the Major retreated to his mirror, at
the back of his apartment for the ostensible purpose of
brushing his whiskers, but in reality to see a reflection of

the lady's face in the glass, when he beheld those eyes, which he had so long sought to look into, meet his gaze and send a sudden pulsation to his heart. He read in their expression much to love and something to hope. When he moved she blushed deeply—her eye-lids fell—and they were friends.

Time vanished—and the Major's funds were also vanishing. Money was nothing to him—love was everything. Three weeks had passed since his first acquaintance with Madame Leech; and yet he had never once suspected that she was the wife of the ex-cashier. He had sought her society, and she was not displeased with his attentions. He read, and laughed, and conversed, and rode with her; but her presence and conversation awed him; for she was "pure as the icicle that hangs from Diana's temple," though not quite as cold. They had rambled together by moonlight through the grove—they stood together upon the banks of the murmuring stream; he drank in the music of her silvery voice, and read poetry in the deep heaven of her eye. But what of that? She was lonely, and wanted society, and no one could be more attentive or agreeable than the Major. How could she refuse? It was plain enough that she had the power of making him happy by her presence, and it was not in her gentle nature to render others unhappy. Moreover, as the lady was most sincerely and devotedly pious, she resolved, in her heart, to be the instrument of his conversion from sin. She was most sincerely anxious about his eternal welfare—there was surely no harm in that.

CHAPTER IX.

A COMPROMISE.

Such was the interesting state of affairs at Badgerton, while, in the meantime, Leech, after having bought an interest in the copper mine of Mr. Jonas, had returned to Galena, where he employed ten miners, with the requisite tools, teams, etc., and proceeded to Little Blue Rabbit, to work out his lead there. Having erected a cabin on the premises, and got everything in readiness for the business, operations were commenced in the grafted mineral hole, by Leech himself. With a new round-topped miner's hat on, he descended with a pick into the hole, and began to drift. In a minute he suspected he was a fool; in another minute he declared he was a fool, and all hands concurred in his opinion. That he was badly duped and wofully taken in and done for, was now palpable. All hands were at once dismissed. Leech mounted his horse and spurred to Badgerton, where he arrived with a face more rueful than a college professor at a faculty meeting during a sophomore rebellion. Counsellor Power was sitting in his office at his desk, with one leg thereon, humming a Scotch air, and musing on the rascality of man in general and of White and Buff in particular, and regreting that he had not taken a hundred dollar fee, when in stepped Leech, with a countenance full of litigation.

"Sir," said the attorney, rising and bowing with much impressment of manner, "I am glad to see you, sir. Please be seated. You must have found it abominable muddy riding—roads are horrible, sir, at present—and *in relation* to the road to Blue Rabbit, I was remarking to our supervisor—"

"That," interrupted Leech, "is the very road I have just traveled."

"Just what I wanted to find out," thought Power. "Now I know you!" Then addressing Leech, quoth he, "Ah? indeed! Anything new at Little Blue Rabbit? I am told there is a fine lead struck?" Thus did the attorney lead the stranger directly to a disclosure of his business.

"Pity said Power, after hearing Leech's tale; "pity," sir, great pity, to go to law. I am free to acknowledge, sir, that you have been somewhat overreached; and indeed I confess I am not fully prepared to deny, that the term *swindled* would be too strong a term to be used in this case. I esteem White a bad man, sir; I do indeed. His conduct is very unwarrantable and reprehensible indeed, sir; and so I shall not hesitate one moment to tell him to his face, sir; that is, if you tell me the truth, which from your appearance, I have no reason in this world to doubt, sir. Neverless, the difficulties of proof, and all the circumstances surrounding the transaction, are of such a nature and character that these considerations, taken in connection with the great uncertainty, the long delay, and the inevitable expense and perplexity of a lawsuit, seems to indicate, that if I were to advise you in this matter, as a friend to all parties concerned, I should, by all means, advise, previous to any coercive measure, that the parties be got together, to try to arrange this difficulty amicably among yourselves."

Accordingly, White and Buff, being sent for, soon made their appearance; Buff in his own attire, and White in a new suit of black, and dressed in admirable style from boot to castor. With the most perfect ease and confidence, Mr.

A COMPROMISE.

White advanced and shook hands with the ex-cashier, who was quite disconcerted with his effrontery. Major White remarked that he was happy to meet Mr. Leech, not having enjoyed that pleasure before, since he had been so foolish as to sell himself out of his lead. Buff being no novice in finesse, sat watching the face of the attorney. Mr. Leech blushed and stammered.

"How," continued White, offering cigars to the company, "how do you find the mineral?"

"Not at all," answered Leech, gruffly, and then whistling as he fixed his eyes on the ceiling over his head.

"What?" said Buff, drawing his feet quickly back, as if about to rise from his chair, and thrusting a hand into each side-pocket of his hairy overcoat, "What?" said he, looking with eyebrows knit at Leech, "What, sir, has the lead petered? Well, well! that is proper bad! We left it right pretty; but prospects is mighty unsartin."

"I believe," said Leech, in a suppppressed tone, which betrayed a violent inward struggle, the pulsations of his heart being audible in the sounds he uttered, "I believe you have colluded and connived together to cheat and defraud me; you are a couple of swindlers, you are."

"Mr. Power," quoth White, raising his hands and looking at the attorney with affected meekness, "Mr. Power, I desire you to notice these certain slanderous and defamatory words, spoken of and concerning us."

"You d —— cut-throat cashier!" growled Buff, springing forward and seizing Leech by the throat; "swallow them are words that you just spit out, or I'll swallow *you* like a Mississippi airthquake."

"Oh! ah! oh!" shrieked Leech; "take him off!"

"Swallow, then!" shouted Buff, choking him.

"Oh! ah! ah! don't cho—oke me!" said Leech. "I swallow. Yes, cer—certainly, I swa—swal—al—allow them."

"Oh! gentlemen! said Power, interfering, "Oh! I beseech you, gentlemen, to desist, or I shall be compelled to arrest you for a breach of the peace."

"Hands off, Buff," said Mr. White, advancing, "let there be no more of this. What does all this mean? For God's sake, let us act like men, and not like dogs. Mr. Leech if you have aught against me, we can settle' amicably, no doubt."

The result of the conference was a final settlement of the difficulty, Leech selling the lead to White, and receiving in full satisfaction of all demands, damages, the sum of two hundred and fifty dollars.

This business over, Mr. Leech, like a dutiful husband, went to see his wife; and she, like any wife, was anxious to know where he had been gone for a month, and what he had been doing.

CHAPTER X.

A CONJUGAL SCENE.

"Mr. Leech, did you bring me the Atlantic Souvenir?"

"No. Where should I find a souvenir to bring you, woman?"

"Why, my dear, I am sure I do not know. That depends upon where you have been. Here you have left me alone amongst strangers for a whole month, without so much as writing me a letter. Pray, what have you been doing?"

"Doing? What the plague is it to a man's wife what he has been doing? Business is business. I'll engage you have not wanted for attentions during my absence. How many suitors have you?"

"For shame, Mr. Leech, to talk so. What cause have I ever given you to make such heartless insinuations?"

The tears glistened in her beautiful eyes. She gazed at the window opposite; her gaze met that of her new friend across the street. She crimsoned, and in a moment her face was all sunshine. She made a sudden resolve, which must remain a secret; told her husband she was to blame—indeed she was—repented, kissed and forgave him; but that night she prayed more fervently than ever for the salvation of her gay young friend across the street, and determined the first favorable opportunity to persuade him to go to the prayer meeting with her.

LOVE REFORMS THE MAN.

It was now winter, and the prairies were robed in snow. The hoary old sun, rising with a brace of sun-dogs, looked across the dazzling expanse of prairie ridges that lay still and unruffled as an ocean of chaos frozen, and saw, as he had for ages seen, the dark channel of the Mississippi, with its branches, like a mammoth tree pictured upon the snowy globe; and smiled upon farms and villages and cities, just created by the magic of steam and civilization, and looked serenely down into the great lakes as into a mirror newly framed, and bordered with the thrift and elegance of civilized society. Far away on the border of many a distant grove, that morning could be seen for the first time the column of blue smoke streaming up from the new lime-painted log cabin; and you could see to count the very logs of which it was the day before constructed, and distinctly hear the axe at the wood pile. It was one of those mornings peculiar to the Northwest, when distance seems to be annihilated, and the power of the senses doubled. It was a dangerous morning for game—whether for the lady-footed deer that congregate in the sunny ravines upon the borders of the leafless grove—or to the platoons of prairie chickens that sit upon a thousand zig-zag rail fences, courting the effulgence of the sun—or to the poor little bare-footed quails that run tripping through the brush like miniature ostriches—or to the hungry wolf that stands upon some bleak knob, and looking impudently back, first over one shoulder and then over the other, challenges the pursuit of the well-mounted horseman.

Such was the morning on which Major James White returned from a hunting excursion of two hours, and dismounted his foaming thorough-bred horse—after riding fifteen or twenty miles, and killing one doe, one wolf and thirteen prairie chickens. During this animated ride, the Major formed a resolution which ever after governed him through life. He determined to be a just man, a just and good man—worthy of the woman he loved. He reflected that much of his money was spent; that was nothing; he believed in his good fortune, and fancied he could strike a lead any day. After breakfast he went to Mr. Leech, and, telling him he had done a wrong and an injury in selling him the prospect, he drew from his purse all the money he had remaining and paid it to the ex-cashier, went home to his room with a light heart, disposed of his horses, dogs, bijouterie, paid all his debts, even his wash bill, informed Buff what he had done, bought Buff's interest in the prospect, hired a digger by the month to work with him, and put on his miner's dress and went back to Little Blue Rabbit to dig again upon his old prospect. He left behind him the following letter addressed to the lady of the ex-cashier:

My Friend—You will look at my window to see me, but you will look in vain. That I love you more dearly than the whole world beside, you know better than I can tell you; how *unworthily* I am to love you, you know not, and heaven only knows. I never knew the blackness of my own heart until I had contrasted it with the purity of yours. You have awed my wayward spirit into the worship of moral beauty. I thank you for it. I now feel compelled by a sense of justice and honor, to surrender my ill-gotten wealth to its rightful owner, and to rely upon honest industry for my support. Dearest woman! with the rising sun, and at noonday, and at twilight, and in the solemn watches of the night, and until the moment we meet again (I hope under happier auspices), your dear image, the angel of my hopes, will ever be living, moving and breathing in the memory of your unworthy friend, JAMES WHITE.

CHAPTER XI.

FINDING A STEADY HOME.

Mr. Leech went to Galena the same day to make preparations for prosecuting business with Mr. Jonas in the Iowa copper mines. But no sooner had he set foot in the Northwestern hotel, than he was seized by an officer by virtue of a warrant and a requisition from the Governor of Michigan, issued on a charge of larceny, for stealing the funds of the Mulberry & Baden Corn Banking Company.

"Mr. Leech," quoth the officer, "you are needed in Michigan!" Leech was alarmed.

"Wh—at is th—at, sir?" said he.

"Why," says the officer, with sham politeness, "If your business here will permit, the Governor of Michigan desires your immediate presence within the limits of that sovereignty."

Accordingly away went the ex-cashier, to answer an indictment of the grand jury of the county of Feline, in the State of Michigan. He wrote not a line to his wife, who had never once suspected him of fraud, and nobody in Galena knew where or why he was gone; and the place that knew the ex-cashier knew him no more forever.

RASCALITY OVERLEAPS ITSELF.

Old Buff took to whisky and smelting. He bought a furnace and might have done well at the business, but having one day taken it into his head that *slag* might be profitably employed by moulding it in the middle of pigs of lead, the honest man, merely by way of experiment, made five hundred pigs of bogus lead, which, somehow or other, through some unaccountable mistake, got into market. The St. Louis purchasers, having detected the blunder, by the breaking of several pigs when unloaded from the boat and thrown upon the pavement, and having ascertained where the mistake originated, made no noise about it, but wrote Mr. Buff the following laconic epistle:

Dear Sir—Many pigs, as we have ascertained, manufactured at your furnace, and bought by us, prove to be *slag veneered* with lead. Supposing that the fraud has been committed by your workmen without your knowledge, we hasten to inform you of the fact (to which we have given no publicity), presuming you will be ready, upon trans-shipment by us of the spurious pigs to Galena, to redeem them in an equal number of good current pigs. We have the honor to subscribe ourselves, sir, your most obedient and humble servants,
GIMLET, VISE & SHARPER.

Accordingly, Messrs. Gimlet, Vise & Sharper, by their first boat, sent up five hundred pigs of bogus lead, which Buff promptly redeemed. The next week they sent seven hundred pigs more, being their whole stock of bogus lead on hand, which had accumulated in the course of several years' trade in lead, but which was manufactured, they knew not where. On the arrival of the second cargo, Buff sweated and swore some; but as he had already redeemed five hundred pigs, he finally thought, to save exposure, he might as well redeem the other seven hundred, although perfectly innocent of emitting them. Thus, moralized Buff, are the innocent sometimes punished for crimes of the guilty.

CHAPTER XII.

CONCERNING WOMEN.

Woman is a paradox—a puzzle. Even Shakespeare was sometimes lost in attempting to trace the labyrinthine mazes of the female heart. It presents more phases and more varied phenomena than anything else in the whole range of nature. This infinite multiformity of woman's character constitutes one of her principal charms. Who has not seen the beautiful combinations of the kaleidoscope? Turn the instrument over. *Now* look! Did you see the transition? No; but I see a new combination, as perfect, as symmetrical, as wonderful as the last. Thus do circumstances and vicissitudes shape and combine and color the character. A woman as changeless as marble would be intolerable; aye, and anomalous; for Lot's wife is the only petrified woman we have any account of. Women allure men by their charms—they soothe them by their kindness—they soften his ferocity by their mildness and affection—they study to render him happy, and they nobly alleviate the burden of his existence—they are full of love and gratitude, but they *will not* be slighted or wronged. They deserve due attention, and they will *command* it. He who leaves his wife, and pays her no more attention than he would an eight-day clock, need not be surprised if, in his absence, she runs down or runs away. My heroine was no longer loved—nay, she was slighted by her husband. She had long repined and suffered, and sought to win his heart. He seemed to be utterly selfish. She had sighed and looked in her mirror, and saw in it her own tall figure—the rounded arm, the tapering hands, the snowy complexion, the auburn ringlets that strayed from under the tiara, the blue eyes melting with love—and she wondered why he, her husband alone, should be insensible to her charms. She wanted some object to love. She had grown melancholy. "To be sure," said she, "I have a friend, whom I prize dearly; he seems like a brother; but it would be wrong for me to love him, as I might if it were not for my marrying vows. How dare I entertain the thought—" Then she sighed again, and looked at the clock, and went to the window to see if her friend were not coming. A servant came in at that moment, and brought the farewell letter from Major White, which we have already presented to the reader. When she had read this letter, the very fountains of her soul seemed broken up. She fell down and wept with uncontrolled agony.

That letter was a key to the mystery of her own heart. Her fancied distinction between friendship and love, vanished; and she found she had long been the victim of the "grand passion."

Perhaps my readers wonder that my heroine is a married lady. That was not my fault. She was never married with *my* consent. This is a new country; and we have to take things as we find them. Then, again, at the time of which I am writing, fine girls were scarce in the mines.—They were mostly plucked in the bud; and no vulgar girl would *do* for the Major. Those days in the mines, like the early days of Rome, were days of violence, when some things were done "contrary to law." Besides, the novelist may create everything to his own liking, if he have invention, but the biographer must confine himself to *facts*.

STRICTLY CONFIDENTIAL.

The following is an exact copy of a letter written at this time by Madame Leech to her bosom friend, in Massachusetts, Miss Florence Hastings, and which I have taken great pains to secure:

DEAREST FLORENCE—Once more let me hold sweet communion with thy spirit. Let my winged thoughts which dare not repose elsewhere, fly back to thy faithful bosom. Or, rather, I will fancy myself, as in days of girlhood, sweet Florence, wandering with you along the bank of the Connecticut in the month of August. It is Saturday evening. Let us be girls again. Let us wear the same calashes and shawls we then wore, and wander along the same meandering path. Here let us be seated once more beneath the venerable elm—this sacred old tree which has sheltered so many generations that are gone, and will drop its rustling leaves, perchance, upon the grave of another century—here let us sit, where we once romanced together. What a holy repose seems to rest upon the face of nature! The shadow of the coming Sabbath rests upon it. Enchanting as ever seems the narrow plain, teeming with golden harvests. The same white cottages and rural towns embowered in ancient shade trees lend tranquil beauty to the landscape. There are still the same cragged old mountains—Mount Tom and Mount Holyoke, with their stern Puritanic features, frowning over the luxuriant plain. Dear Florence! These recollections make me sad. Let us sit down and commune together. I cannot imagine that you are changed since I saw you—that you are not the same artless young girl that you were, but as you part my auburn tresses again, I fancy I hear you say, "Mary, here is sorrow penciled on thy brow, and thine eye looks more experienced—but oh! forgive me! not more *pure*." I *do* forgive thee, Florence; but can I forgive myself? I have learned, my dear girl, too late, that I do not love the man to whom I am married. I strove to love him. It was impossible. I did not know the meaning of the word *love*—much less had I ever felt the all controlling power of that passion. My husband was much absent—indeed, has scarcely pretended to remain at home since we moved from Michigan. Circumstances threw me into the society of a young man of my own age—a man of fine address, of education, and wit—but of rather dissolute habits. I was pleased with his society—I found in him nobler qualities than perhaps the world knew he possessed—I sought to reclaim him. He listened to my persuasions. I, too, listened to the narrative of his adventures in life. He talked to me of the mountains and golden plains of Mexico—described the gorgeous city of the Montezumas—told me of the Alamo, and of the perils of San Jacinto—

and I listened, oh! too fondly listened, and, like Desdemona, sighed and wondered, and "wished that heaven had made me such a man." Florence, I loved and still do love him. Oh! pardon, forgive your erring friend! Thus far am I fallen. Oh! the omnipotence of love! I knew not what it was; I thought it was *friendship*, until he was gone; then, when I listened for music, the harp was broken—when I looked for support, his arm was not there to lean upon—when I looked for light, there was only darkness. When I looked for him and saw him not—when I listened for him and he came not, but sent a farewell, I awoke from the delusion. I have struggled to forget him. What am I to do? Ruin surrounds me. What is character? what is honor—what is life without him? Dearest Florence! If you have loved as I love, you will answer—nothing, nothing. Oh! I could moralize once. I could talk of self-respect and pride and decorum. These motives may weigh with those who do not need their restraint; but I—I, who love him alone, and have my thoughts, feelings, affections and almost my existence, identified with his—I may *perish*—perhaps in disgrace—but never shall his dear image be torn from my heart.

Florence, I am far away from you in the land of gigantic rivers and boundless prairies. I sometimes hope that I may yet be happy. I have a thousand things to tell you, and a thousand questions to ask you when I embrace you again, if ever.

Your affectionate friend,
MARY M. LEECH.

P. S.—In your next, please inform me whether "Orientalaines" is as much worn for dresses as ever; and whether "a la Pacha" is worn by the recherche? M. M. L.

CHAPTER XIII.

STRIKING THE MAIN BODY AHEAD.

Mr. White went forty feet due east of the grafted mineral hole, and there commenced sinking another shaft ; working in the shaft himself—for he rightly judged that the hired man would be less likely to break the Major's head through carelessness at the windlass, than "to cover up mineral on him," if allowed to work in the ground, On the third day at noon, they had sunk forty feet down to a cap-rock that covered the whole width of the crevice. After dinner, Mr. White drilled into the rock thirteen inches, and put in a blast of powder, which shivered the rock to fragments. The pieces of rock fell through into a cavity beneath. Upon going down, Mr. White found he had opened into an immense cavern of ore, with a space of six feet between the mineral and cap rock. He sent for a candle and matches, and explored the cavern east one hundred and fifty yards; walking all the way over a turnpike of mineral. Elated with his discovery, he returned to the opening, and fastened the rope with a noose around one of the fragments of rock, and ordered the windlass man to hoist it. Not anticipating the least danger, Mr. White, instead of stepping aside into the cavern, remained at the bottom of the shaft. When the rock was raised a part of the way up, the rope broke and the rock fell upon his back, grazing the back part of his head, and knocking him senseless. Help obtained he was carried to his cabin nearly dead. Medical aid was sent for, and two doctors came. The two doctors were of different schools in the art of killing. One of them slew his patients with calomel and the lancet, while the other finished them with lobelia and red pepper, and stifled them in steam. They held a consultation; that was a critical time for Mr. White. Dr. Lancet was proceeding to bleed. Dr. Lobelia protested against it.

"The patient requires," said the professor of phlebotomy, "immediate and copious depletion, to relieve the pressure of blood from the brain. He is already in a comatose state."

"The patient requires no such thing," quoth Lobelia. "The blood is the life; and the man is nearly dead already. He requires something warming, and nourishing, and stimulating to keep the breath of life in him."

"You talk like a fool!" rejoined Lancet. What do you know of the human system? You cannot tell on which side of a patient the heart lies. I am sometimes charged with exaggeration, but I will take my oath you have too little knowledge of anatomy to cut a patient's finger nails."

"You lie!" retorted Lobelia; "and you are a lying trifling puppy, you are. You mow down mankind like a simoon, and your track is like the tornado. You have peopled more than ten quarter sections of grave-yards, and fed out more of your nasty *poison calomy* than ten grist mills could grind. *You* pretend to be a surgeon! Why you are not fit to tap a seed cucumber for dropsy! *You* a doctor? You don't know the itch from the small pox. But you can out-lie me, and I give it up."

Accordingly Major White was freely bled; and, to tell the truth, he was certainly benefitted by the operation. Dr. Lancet went home; but Dr. Lobelia staid at Blue Rabbit until midnight; for he was determined to "crack down" on the patient himself, with steam. He was just preparing to administer to the patient an injéction of cayenne, when he was interrupted in the manner I will now proceed to relate.

A FRIEND IN NEED.

Oh! what is love made for, if it is not the same
Through joy and through sorrow, through glory and shame?
I know not, I asked not, if guilt's in that heart,
But I know that I love thee, whatever thou art!

Thou hast call'd me thy angel in moments of bliss;
Still thy angel I'll be 'mid the horrors of this;
Thro' the furnace unshrinking thy steps to pursue,
And shield thee, and save thee, or perish there too!

MOORE.

Oh! woman! What can equal the moral sublimity of thy spirit? Whether thou art found in the the tent of the wild Arab, or in the wigwam of the Indian, or cradled in the luxuries of palaces, or sharing the toils and dangers of the western pioneer, thy free, noble daring, and enduring spirit ever glistens like the polar star in the dark hour of man's adversity.' Though the heartless sneer at thee, and the cold and selfish deride thy sufferings and thy sacrifices, thou art ready, if need be, to suffer all and to endure all, at the shrine of thy heart's devotion.

The first news the wife of the ex-cashier had of Mr. White, after he departed from Badgerton, was that he lay at the point of death, some fifteen miles distant, at Little Blue Rabbit. Then it was that the mighty impulses of woman's sympathy were aroused in her gentle bosom. Before then, all softness and weakness, she was now in a moment nerved with the firmness of iron. She instantly formed a high resolve, which, like a resistless torrent, bore down all fear of danger or obstacles—all pride—all conventional notions of decorum; all the the impulses of her heart were merged in one purpose—to go that very night and alleviate the dying sufferings of her young friend, whose unredeemed soul was hovering on the brink of eternity. Despatch and profound secrecy were requisite. For the first time in her life she robed her delicate limbs in male attire, which she contrived to obtain. She left a billet upon her writing desk, addressed to her sister, informing her that she was summoned suddenly away and would return in a few days, and imploring her not to be alarmed at her sudden departure—the cause of which she would hereafter explain. Her nimble little feet were soon on the road to Little Blue Rabbit. Her only guide across the snowy expanse of moonlight prairie was a distant mound, the outline of which was distinctly pictured against the blue sky; and which she knew was near the place she sought to find.

About midnight a gentle rap was heard at the door of the patient's cabin. A rough miner came and opened the door. The graceful stranger entered, and tripped lightly to the bed of the sufferer. He was groaning deeply and lay entirely unconscious of all around him.

After a few moments, her eye seemed to kindle with new hope and resolution. "What are you doing for the patient?" inquired the graceful stranger, addressing Dr. Lobelia.

"Why," said the doctor, "I have placed two hot bricks at his feet and given him the Composition and some warm Lobelia tea to nourish his stomach—and I am going to give him an—

"Enough, doctor," interrupted the blushing youth. "I have to inform you that I am this patient's nearest friend. Make out your bill. Your further services can be dispensed with." The stranger spoke as one not to be trifled with;

and Doctor Lobelia was taken with a leaving. She then removed the two hot bricks and applied cold water freely to the patient's head, and she administered such other palliatives as common sense seemed to indicate, and watched over him with constant tenderness, until the arrival of Dr. Lancet. On examination of the patient's hat, it appeared that his skull had been shielded from fracture, by some papers that happened to be in his hat, and which papers she ventured to take the custody of. One of the papers was an open half sheet, on which were written with a pencil, the following lines; which as they were interesting to her are here transcribed.

> When he whose feverish brain gives birth
>   To fond thoughts written here,
> Is torn from all he loves on earth,
>   Oh! drop for him a tear.
>
> This throbbing pulse, this feverish frame,
>   Betray my secret soul,
> And tell that her I dare not name,
>   I love beyond control.
>
> Perchance no more thy form divine
>   My watchful eyes shall bless;
> Yet, though thou never canst be mine,
>   I cannot love thee less.
>
> The stream, the plain, the prairie flower,
>   Each object that I see,
> And every moment of each hour
>   My memory links to thee.

She watched over the sufferer until the fourth night and until his reason began to revive and he was pronounced free from danger, when with a blush she imprinted an impassioned kiss upon his forehead and departed. The next morning she came down from her room to breakfast at her sister's at the usual hour.

CHAPTER XIV.

PLANTING A SUIT.

Calamities are gregarious and come mostly in flocks. No sooner was Major White on his feet again, than he was threatened with a leash of law suits. First came old Buff—who insisted that his partnership with the Major had never been dissolved; and demanded one-half of the lead. He was soon quieted, however. "Never mention it to me again, Buff," said the Major, pale with anger, and touching the hilt of his six-shooter, "never name partnership to me again, you dishonest old rascal. Five words more from you, would tempt me to blow your brains out. Look me in the eye, you brazen old knave, and tell me how you dare attempt to practice this impudent rascality upon me."

Old Buff's eye quailed. He looked upon the ground and commenced stirring the dust with the toe of his boot. At length he said, in a subdued tone, that he wanted money.

"You shall have money," quoth the Major. "But if you have money off me, you must take it as a gift and not demand it as a right."

Smith and Hawkins, who the reader will recollect, long since jumped the diggings, set up a much more formidable claim to the Major's discovery; for they had been in peaceable possession of the range running east, ever since the grafting of the mineral hole; and had raised several thousand of top mineral; though they had never yet gone down into the underbody of ore.

They employed as their attorneys, Messrs. Shave & Still.

"State your case gentlemen," said Shave to his clients; for

Shave did all the talking, while Still held his tongue, and got credit for keeping up a devil of a thinking.

Bill Smith went on to state that he and his partner commenced digging on the range on the 21st day of October— that then there was no discovery made on the ground; that Buff and White had then pretended to make a discovery, but that in point of fact they had only grafted their mineral hole; that they, Smith and Hawkins, had struck mineral the very day Leech purchased of Buff and White—that White had since bought out Leech and Buff, and gone ahead on the crevice east, and struck it big.

"One of you," quoth Shave, "must sell out his interest to the other, and come in as a witness, if we proceed for a forcible entry and detainer."

Mr. Still nodded assent.

"And," continued Shave, "you must get old Buff and train *him*. He will be a material witness."

Mr. Still nodded approbation.

"We must bring the suit—let me see—where *will* we bring the suit? There is Esquire Green—he is right—and the next nearest justice of the peace before whom the cause could be moved is Esquire Gosling, and he is right, too; yes, we will commence before Green. Now for the jury. "There is," said Shave, counting his fingers, "there is Cringe, who stands indicted of hog stealing, is one; Cotton, against whom we have a judgment, makes two; Swallow, who believes in all that Green says, makes three; Shallow, who swears that you are the deepest lawyer in the Territory, makes four; Whimper, the man I defended for flogging his wife, makes five; Dig, who don't like any body should be too lucky, makes six; Nuckle, who believes in majorities, makes seven; Hungry, who never hangs a jury, makes eight; Wrede, who wants to do what the majority think right, makes nine; Guzzle, who says he can see no sense in requiring a jury to drink water only, makes ten; and as for the balance, it can be made up of ciphers. We must carry out a load of loafers for the talesmen."

CHAPTER XV.

THE TEA PARTY.

Although we western folks mostly drink coffee, the tea party has found its way here; and the tea market of the celestial empire widens in the circle of civilization that is spreading over our hemisphere. We are too mercurial to drink coffee alone, and to be taciturn as Turks. We want tea as scandal—it is our birthright—and we *will* have it.

One after another of the ladies of Badgertown dropped into the house of Mrs. Tibbets. Each lady came with but little bustle (for bustles were yet in embryo) but they had each a *boa* entwining her neck—a fashion as old, for what I know, as Eve. There was but little "music" until after each lady had imbibed three cups of "imperial." After tea the sweet fountains of loquacity (and some not so sweet) were opened, and there was an inundation of small talk—a perfect deluge of scandal, which threatened the destruction of every character out of their "ark."

"You don't say it!" quoth Miss Stubbs.

"What? Two wives living!" exclaimed Mrs. Grubbs.

"Abominable creature!" exclaimed Miss Stubbs.

"Won't the grand jury *interdict* him?" inquired Mrs. Snubbs.

"If *I* were his wife and he should throw the sugar bowl at *my* head," quoth Mrs. Drubbs; a sharp nosed termagant, "he would *catch* it, I'll warrant you; I would get him rode on a rail, I would."

"Yeth," said little Miss Coombs, lisping, "yeth, it ith my imprethion that I would return railing for railing, too.

The conversation here arose into a confused murmur—a sort of parlor Babel—a conglomeration of sentences knocked into "pi," which at length subsided into a calm; when all at once a fresh buzzing was heard in one corner, which presently broke into a distinct whisper between Miss Celia Parsimmon and Miss Abigail Cauliflower.

"In a *man's* clothes?" inquired Miss Parsimmon, dropping her sewing into her lap, and raising both hands with a look of horror.

"Yes," replied aunt Abigail, looking out sternly over her spectacles and speaking more audibly; "yes, and in the night, too."

"Where?" "Which way?" "Who?" "What?" "When?" "Who is it?" "Where was it?" "How was it?" exclaimed a dozen at once.

"I shall call no names," answered Miss Cauliflower. "You must take it just as I got it. The woman is a stranger here. *Perhaps* they were very nice people in Michigan; but when a woman's husband is gone, for her to leave home all of a sudden and not be seen again for four days and nights, and finally to come home again all stark alone when it is pitch dark, in a man's clothes, I don't think it very *prudent* if she *is* a cashier's wife.

To do the ladies justice, there was a majority who refused to give the tale any credence. They said that Madame Leech had every appearance of being a lady, and would not believe any such scandalous story—and that if there was any semblance of foundation for it, they thought it might be explained so as to be consistent with her purity. A division of opinion arose—and all voices chimed in to swell the chorus of queries and interjections; so that there was a noise in Mrs. Tibbet's parlor for about the same length of time that St. John says three was silence in heaven; viz: for about the space of half an hour, by Mrs. Tibbet's new brass clock. A dumb tea party would be profitable for exhibition; and amongst a thousand arguments to prove that the gentle sex share with man, hereafter, that heaven, which, with all their faults, they so much more richly merit, none perhaps is more conclusive than the negative proof furnished in the text: "There was silence in heaven for about the space of half an hour"—a fact that never would have been deemed worthy of record, had heaven been peopled only by our own saturine sex.

CHAPTER XVI.

TURNING OVER A NEW LEAF.

Opposition or antagonism is the main spring of creation. The concussion of the flint and steel produces fire—the collision of mind produces wit—from the meeting of the opposite sexes result the mighty stream of original existence—opposition multiplies steamboats, accelerates speed and reduces rates—opposition multiplies merchants and mechanics, lawyers and litigation—opposition made Mr. Van Buren president and Napoleon Bonaparte emperor—opposition stimulated Philip of Macedon to play the hero, and inspired Demosthenes to thunder forth his Phillippics—opposition planted Nauvoo, like a cancer, on the bosom of the Mississippi and pimpled the whole valley of the west with rival churches — opposition reduced the price of brogans and built up the rival towns of Rock Island and Davenport, and opposition drives out the very dogs of those two respective villages to howl defiance at each other by moonlight across the cold shining river. Rivalry and competition stimulate the active millions that are swarming over this new continent. ˙ The great globe itself blooming afresh with every annual revolution, were it not for the antagonism of the centrifugal and centripedal forces, would cease its glorious career and would fall into lifeless, formless, chaos. There seems to be two opposite principles of mind, the conflict of which is essential to call into exercise all the faculties and to develop all the capabilities of our nature. If these opposite principles be weak the character will be feeble. "Confound your harmless folks," as a lady of wit and beauty once remarked. Better to be wavering and inconstant than to be nobody.

Several circumstances had lately combined to call into exercise the better principle of Major White's nature and to effect a change in his character. The injury upon his head so nearly fatal, had led him to reflect on the shortness and uncertainty of life, as yet neither useful nor virtuous. His pecuniary circumstances were now such as placed him above the temptation to steal. He found himself suddenly a man of some importance and felt a growing self-respect and pride of character. But his passion for the elegant woman whom he idolized, more than all other causes had been instrumental in purifying the fountains of his heart and ennobling his soul. No man is irreclaimable who is capable of sincerely and devotedly loving a woman of purity and refinement. Men of dissolute *habits* may love—men of dissolute *hearts* cannot. Those polished scoundrels who "drag angels down" generally pass for men of good morals. There is hope for those who are not too selfish to look up and be guided by "some bright particular star." Love assimilates those who exercise it perhaps by some law of physical affinities better understood by Professor De Bonneville than by the writer. Major White's resolution to reform was also strengthened by the following letter from his parents:

CLOCKTON, Conn., Jan. 10, 184—.

MY SON:—So then you are in Wisconsin? Where in the world have you been for these ten years? James, James, you are old enough to be a man. What on earth is the reason you could not stay at home and be steady and enjoy the ordinances of the gospel, like your younger brother, John, who is now settled at Ragton, and owns a large cotton factory, and is one of the pillars in Dr. Brimstone's church and society? You was always a wayward boy and required frequent chastisement. Consecrated as you were in childhood, by the holy ordinance of baptism, I could not believe that you would wander away from this land of gospel light and liberty, and spend your days in the darkness of heathenism, amongst pagans, infidels and Catholics. You have had all the advantages which education could bestow. I have expended thousands for your instruction. You had from childhood wholesome family discipline, and you were required to listen to the lively oracles of God. You were faithfully taught the decalogue and catechism, too, of the assembly of holy Westminster divines. In due time you were sent to a good sound orthodox New England college, where you graduated. I had fondly hoped, my son, that your mind might be awakened to a realizing sense of your lost and undone condition, and, after three years of study at the Andover Theological Seminary, you might become a herald of the cross and proclaim the tidings of salvation from the pulpit. How great has been my disappointment! You left home; nothing could induce you to stay; and after ten years I have the *satisfaction* to learn that you have been a ragged Texan Major, and that you are now at large in the Northwest without property, family or character! Glorious cause and most noble destiny!—to have spent the prime of your life in fighting for the sham democrats of Texas, who are gloating upon the blood of the slave. Pray, what is your Texan emblem bird? A buzzard! Oh, my son! such conduct is heinous enough to call down the wrath of heaven and to arouse the very ashes of your Pilgrim fathers. Your mother will conclude this letter.

JOHN WHITE, SR.

P. S.—Inclosed find a check for one hundred dollars. Come home immediately.

MY LONG LOST SON:—In what shall your mother now address her first-born? Are you, indeed, my veritable child? Months and years have rolled by since your departure. Year followed year and brought no tidings of you until you were remembered only as one of the dead. Oh! I have seen you in a thousand dreams; in peril—in pomp—in boyhood—in manhood—in all conceivable circumstances of existence. Sitting alone by the hearth where you were cradled, and listening to the mournful chorus of the crickets, I have often fancied I have heard the voice of my lost boy calling me in unforgotten tones. Oh, my son! myself! dearer to me than the light of heaven which I first saw dawn upon your infant eyes! What anguish have I not felt for you? I thank God you cannot know. No, no; none but a mother can know anguish. At last news of you came. Mr. Robert Acres, a speculator in Western lands, being at a party at our house on Thanksgiving evening, informed us of you. Your father, whose head is now silvered with age, and your brothers and sisters also, unite with me in requesting your immediate return home. That my prayers to God with you and for you have been answered in the salvation of your soul and preservation of your honor untarnished—and that you may return a Christian and a gentleman—but above all that you may *return* to these arms that encircled you in your infancy, is the earnest petition of your poor mother.

MARIA WHITE.

CHAPTER XVII.

MESMERISM.

The Major was troubled. There was the anxiety of his friends at home about his welfare, and particularly the earnest appeal of his mother, whom he loved, tenderly; then the difficulties, expenses, and risk of a lawsuit in defense of his discovery; but more than all, the agony of separation from the lady he loved. All these causes had combined to depress his spirits, and produce melancholy. At times, he almost repented of his resolution to sacrifice his attachment to the lady, dishonorable though its indulgence might prove, and ruinous to them both. It is highly probable, in this irresolute state of mind, that, if he had believed the lady would play Cleopatra, he would have enacted Mark Antony. But whenever he considered his cash account, his virtue recovered its wonted equilibrium. Now, the Major, to be secure from temptation, had resolved to return no more to Badgerton; but business now required him to go there, and he went.

It was Saturday evening when he arrived in that beautiful little village, and stopped at the best hotel; but which hotel that was, I have not ascertained. Everybody had gone to attend a lecture on the novel science of Mesmerism; and, after tea, having nothing else to do, the Major went likewise. Even Madame Leech, dejected and melancholy as she was, had, at the earnest solicitation of her sister, taken a seat in the crowded audience, to listen to the peripatetic philosopher. The Major entered the room and uncovered his intellectual brow, and took a seat near the lecturer. He was, for a moment, the cynosure of all eyes; but one there was who, when she glanced at him, started as if an arrow had reached her heart; but he knew not of her presence.

How is philosophy fallen! Shades of Newton and Franklin and Spurzheim, your mantles have fallen upon the shoulders of mountebanks.. Here was a teacher of philosophy who had certainly blundered into some of the sublimest mysteries of physiology, which he exhibited to the conviction of the most skeptical; yet, when he undertook to explain the wonderful phenomena, and prate about the "*lors* of nature," he only proved himself to be a fool. He was like a child that had thrust a lever into some complicated machine, and arrested its motion for the examination of others; but of the construction of which he was himself more ignorant than any spectator, and was as unfit to teach philosophical *theories*, as was the silken cord with which Franklin, as with a lariat, noosed and dragged down the lingering lightnings from their wild home in heaven.

"Here," said the lecturer, turning to Major White, "here is a gentleman of a temperament that I never fail to bring under Mesmeric influence. If I am not mistaken in his appearance, he is a somnambulist. If he will consent to be mesmerized, I think I will afford the audience some very pretty exhibitions of clairvoyance."

The Major smiled incredulously, and at the urgent solicitation of Mr. Power and several other gentlemen, consented to the experiment. The lecturer took a seat facing the subject, and looked him steadily in the eye for about five minutes. The subject at length began to perceive a misty veil spreading before his vision—he grew unconscious of what was passing around him. The lecturer then approached him, and gently closed the lids of his eyes, drew his fingers lightly over him a few times from the head downward—then pressed his hand upon the subject's bosom. The subject's senses were locked in profound slumber—his cheek was flushed—his pulse was quickened—and his limbs were rigid. The hushed audience breathed again.

"Now," said the lecturer, "I will excite the subject's organ of memory, and try to ascertain what is most indelibly impressed upon it."

He touched the organ of memory.

"Oh!" groaned the somnambulist, "it was a terrible blow! I fear, doctor, the skull is fractured. Thus, then, I am to perish—and where is she? Oh! may she never, never know my fate!"

"Can any one explain the meaning of this language?" asked the lecturer.

"Yes," said Mr. Power, "he was nearly killed not long since, by the falling of a rock on his head in a mining hole. This is one of my clients, sir, Major White, of Blue Rabbit."

"Ah!" said the lecturer, "that is a key to this subject's mind. His brain has been more or less injured; and hence his amazing susceptibility to this influence. I will now excite amativeness in connection with memory, and see if I can learn anything about his lady-love."

All this time Madame Leech was sitting motionless as a statue, with her eyes riveted upon the subject.

Memory and amativeness were now excited.

"Oh! thou angel of light!" exclaimed the subject; his face beaming with eloquence; "hast thou indeed come, mistress of my soul, to minister to my dying agonies in this dungeon? Do I not know thy foot-fall—thy voice—thy dove-like eye, through all disguises? Dream of heaven, vanish not!"

All were astonished. An emotion of sublimity was felt by all; for each one was conscious that he was looking into the very mystery of our nature.

"Now," said the lecturer, "we will see if this subject can be made prophetic."

The proper organs being excited, the lecturer asked the subject if he could see anything in the future.

"Yes."

"What do you see?"

"I see upon the prairie, a log cabin, and stable, and stacks, and men and wagons; two horses that cannot move."

"What are they doing in the house? What do you see there."

"Many people are there; and a new clock, and a great fire-place, a bed, and trundle-bed full of children."

"Travel on—what else do you see?"

"I see two men running in a snowstorm on the prairie— one of them I think is Buff."

"Where are they gone?"

"There! they have dropped out of sight! I cannot see them any more."

"This is an intellectual man," said the lecturer— perhaps a poet. Let us see what may be the effect of exciting ideality, amativeness, tune, language, and cautiousness. I include cautiousness for fear the subject may improperly betray some secret of his own."

When these organs were excited, the subject stood up, and at the same instant, as if moved by the same impulse, the lady of the ex-cashier also arose, to the astonishment of everybody. The subject then proceeded to utter, with the most fervid and impassioned elocution, the following stanzas. Meanwhile the lady stood in the attitude of a listener, with her eyes riveted upon the subject, her right foot advanced—her fore-finger raised—her lips apart, like a statue growing into life:

> Deep in the heaven of her eye
>   Love sat enthroned;
> I gazed—I knelt—and with a sigh
>   Love's power I owned;
> But she was not my own—
> Her name must be unknown.
>
> I listened to her syren voice—
>   It thrilled my very soul;
> I loved her, though another's choice,
>   Beyond control.
> Still she was not my own—
> Her name must be unknown.
>
> Her foot-fall made my pulses dance
>   When she drew nigh;
> We crimsoned at each other's glance,
>   Yet dared not sigh;
> For she was not my own—
> Her name must be unknown.
>
> Our straying fingers, trembling met,
>   One summer night;
> We glowed with burning rapture; yet
>   It was not right;
> For she was not my own—
> Her name must be unkhown.
>   * * * * *
> * * * * * ⁁ ⁂ * *

"Astonishing!" "Most wonderful!" were the exclamations of every one. "Ladies and gentlemen," said the lecturer, these are the most astonishing phenomena I ever witnessed. Here seems to be two subjects. Let me examine this lady." Upon examination it appeared, sure enough, that the two were in a state of deep somnolency. Her limbs were rigid, her respiration was difficult, and her immovable eyes were fixed upon the other subject. The operator waved his hand upward, near her person, reversing the magnetizing process, when, behold, both the lady and the gentleman, at the same instant, looked around them with wild expressions of returning reason, and sat down among the astonished spectators entirely unconscious of their experience while under the influence of mesmerism.

A MINERAL SERMON.

The next day was Sunday, and the Major went to meeting, as every gentleman should do. No class of men perhaps in the world, more need the restraint of the gospel than the miners. The greater part of them are young men, removed from the influence of parents, and untamed by the magic charm of female society. The miner is frequently found a man of great daring, of much generosity, and wonderful force of character; but generally improvident, and too often with a dash of ferocity in him that rides rough-shod over the requisite restraint of law or order. Here, if anywhere, the pulpit should be supplied with eloquent and learned—aye, *learned* divines; devout men, whose morals will endorse their doctrines, and whose dress and address will correspond to the dignity of their profession.

The Major glanced around to see if he could discover amongst the worshippers, her whose eye beaming with love had so often sent through him a sudden thrill of ecstacy. There was a galaxy of bright eyes, flashing and twinkling around him; but those bright particular stars that ruled his destiny, were invisible. Where is *she?* Perhaps at some other place of worship; for he that would see the entire array of beauty, in this village, must look two ways of a Sunday, or perhaps—but a truce to conjectures. Service commenced—the prayer was ended—and the hymn was sung. The preacher stood up in the pulpit, a man of forty years of age, clad in a rather slovenly suit He had a face as imperturbable as cast-iron, and lungs like a mule. "The text may be found in Proverbs, the second chapter and the fourth verse, in these words: 'If thou seekest her as silver, and searchest for her as for hid treasures.' My dear hearers: In the text widsom is personified and put in the feminine gender, to be the more attractive.— Wisdom, wearing whiskers like a boat-swain, would fail to win your hearts, and you would shun rather than seek for it.

"Now, then, how are you to seek for wisdom? Why just as you would dig for a lead—that is, you must keep popping down after it. Judea was probably a mining region, and hence this simile, borrowed from the mines, naturally occurred to Solomon. I shall not here attempt to philosophise upon the origin of mineral, nor make a geological inquiry concerning its formation. It is immaterial whether it has ben forced up through fissures and crevices in the shell of the earth by internal heat, or whether it is formed in the great laboratory of nature, by chemical combinations of earths—whether it grows by mere accretion, or whether it has an organization and principle of vitality in it, analagous to a bed of oysters. The simplest and best theory I know of is this. That the same God, who in the beginning said, 'let there be light, and there was light,' said 'let there be mineral,' and there was mineral. The formation of mineral is no more mysterious than the formation of marble.

Well; no matter how it came where it is, so long as we find it in divers and sundry places, wedged in between the ribs of the earth, and can sell it for fifteen dollars a thousand, men *will* prospect. Oh! that they should search for wisdom, as for this hidden treasure! Men who prospect, dig where there are the best signs of mineral. They sink in some of the general North and South ranges of east and west crevices. They would no sooner go between these ranges to get mineral, than I would go to a ball-room to get wisdom.— Again, the miner keeps the tools to work with; but how many of you are destitute of that great instrument of salvation, the Bible? The miner watches the signs—observes the float—notices the color of the ochre and the pitch of the clay; but, alas! how few of you watch the emotions of your hearts—search for the internal signs of spiritual wisdom, or notice the pitch of your affections. In your search for mineral you penetrate through flint—you raise tumbling rock— you blast the solid cap rock—you tear out the very bowels of the earth; but in digging for wisdom, how easily you are discouraged by the slightest obstacles. When the miner makes a discovery, he knows what he has found, and never mistakes black-jack for mineral; but how many fancy they have experienced religion, and found the treasure of eternal wisdom, are in fact only working out fanaticism and folly. Ah! my hearers; how infinitely more valuable is wisdom, than the richest cavern of sparkling ore. If you find wisdom it cannot be 'jumped away' from you, and you can never be 'lawed' out of it. The great enemy of souls may indeed sometimes cut your windlass rope, or dull your tools, or let the water into your shaft: but you have only to splice your rope—sharpen your tools and work the pump of prayer. You cannot be robbed of your discovery; and you shall find more and more wisdom until it runs on as big as mules; and when all other leads have failed—when this earth shall become one vast furnace—and when all the ore in her veins shall have melted and trickled down in bright silver streams into the boiling rivers and steaming oceans—and when the elements themselves shall melt with fervent heat, your treasure of eternal wisdom shall still be within your grasp,

During the last of the singing, our hero was placed in a dilemma. He saw a contribution-box travelling towards him. He had no money with him but two twenty dollar Missouri bills. Now, said he, what am I to do? Sit here the observed of all, and refuse to contribute anything? or sacrifice all to pride? Let them go by; if they wish to lay a soul-excise, they should at least give gentlemen notice. Who could anticipate, that these good folks who make such an outcry against carrying the mail and raising incidental revenue from the Post-Office on Sunday, would select that very day for the express purpose of levying a direct soul-tax!

CHAPTER XVIII.

TAKING THE BENEFIT.

A lawsuit may be a pleasant thing, that is to say, provided one is not elected defendant. It is really a satisfaction to assist those whose legal rights are invaded, if one gets *paid* for it; for the lawyer who hires himself out, like a Swiss soldier, to battle for his client right or wrong, must have the recompense of reward. The people seem to have grown insensible to their rights, and suffer them to be trampled upon with impunity. Let the millenium or the small pox stalk before the public gaze, and everybody grows as meek as Moses; the fires of resentment burn down, until there is scarcely heat enough left to keep the old chancery caldrons simmering. When Death or the Cholera are holding their assizes, our practice yields to that of the medical faculty. We do not complain at this; " live and let live " is our motto; though some of the doctors do not subscribe to it. The bankrupt law has swept away much of the material of litigation. Like the rod of Moses, it was stretched across the sea of debts and obligations, and that sea yawned open to its slimy bottom, and the beggarly host of debtors marched through carrying away in triumph their creditors' " jewels of silver and jewels of gold, and rainment." They are now winding away into the wilderness, to raise straw and make bricks for themselves; and our vocation of taskmaster is gone. It reminds one of the boy who killed the goose. We have had the satisfaction of dining upon a *lean goose;* but what are we to do now for *eggs?* Think of that Mr. Power. Buff was getting embarrassed. His old " Drummond " furnace had cost him a large sum in repairs—his smelters had failed to obtain a good per centum from his mineral—his bogus lead operation had cost him some money and shaken his credit—his grocery bills were large—and another installment had become due upon the purchase of his furnace. Unable to get an advance of money in Galena, he went to Badgerton, to try to effect a loan upon a mortgage of his furnace and for this purpose he called upon Counsellor Power.

"You say," quoth Power, "that you must have eighty-five dollars?"

"That are a fact."

"Is that all you owe?"

"Yes, it are, except my liquor bills."

"Could you not conscientiously make oath that you are unable to meet your debts and obligations?"

"Bekase why?"

"Because, if you could, you might take the benefit."

"Take what?"

"Take the benefit, Mr. Buff; that is, the benefit of the bankrupt act, for such case made and humanely provided. That is, you will get a free discharge from all your debts."

"Take the oath? . Well, I could, hoss. I can't raise the eighty-five dollars, no how I can fix it—thirty is all I can raise in the ready."

"I will get your discharge for thirty dollars or thereabouts. You will have to advance, from time to time, the clerk's and printer's fees. Mind you, I do not *advise* you to take the benefit. I act entirely upon your suggestions."

"But my furnace?"

"Your creditors will never prove up a dollar of their demands against you; and you can bid in your furnace at the assignee's sale for three bits."

"What personal property have you, Mr. Buff?"

"Three pistols, a bowie knife, and my other necessary wearing apparel."

"Ahem! Well, Buff, the law will allow you this sort of necessary personal property to the amount of two or three hundred dollars."

"No! Well, if so be that mought be the case, I will in the first place go and run my face with Slop for three new suits of clothes and a hickory shirt."

"Have you no other personal property? Have you no gun or watch?"

"Well, I haven't; but I know where I can buy both on credit."

"Where is that fine red trotting horse you had of Major White?"

"Swallowed," said Buff; opening his huge jaws, and pointing down his red throat; drunk up squire—gone down, hoof and tail; but I have a poor little filley, and a saddle and bridle, that you may have after I have rode her to the forcible entry suit next week."

"Thank you, thank you, Mr. Buff; I was just going to remark in relation to the filley, that you could have no earthly use for her."

Before the next week, sure enough, Buff was added to the list of unfortunate petitioners in bankruptcy. He shone out in a new wardrobe, and laughed at sheriffs, courts and constables.

RATHER A DELICATE AFFAIR.

Major White went to consult his attorney. He found Power at his office in "Doggery lane"—a street narrower than the road to heaven.

"Of course Mr. Power," said he, "I wish you to defend this suit for me; and if it will be agreeable to you, sir, I will have Mr. Quibble associated with you. Whatever attempts the other party may make to suborn Buff, I have nothing to fear from him. I know him well; and he knows and fears *me*. If sworn, I have no doubt but he will tell exactly the truth. I hope our rascally transaction with Leech may not transpire in evidence."

"Very well," answered Power, "that is well. Buff alone knows of that transaction, and he will not convict himself. Bring a copy of the writ, when served, if you please. Now then, in relation to that other business, Major, I have, as you suggested, written to Michigan, from whence I learn, that the rumor you heard at Galena was not unfounded. I have here authentic proof that Leech is sentenced to the penitentiary; but if the election for governor of that State terminate as may be feared, he will probably be pardoned."

The Major's face turned instantly pale—then it was flushed; and fairly trembling with excitement, he arose and rapidly paced the office.

"No!" he exclaimed, with great emphasis. "Then she shall be mine! God I thank thee! Tell me, is there no hope? Is not his imprisonment a good ground for her divorce? Talk to me! For God's sake, tell me!"

"Why," said the attorney, "it may be done by a bill in chancery; but it will take at least six months to obtain a decree."

"For which your fee would be how much?"

"Fifty dollars."

"Is there no shorter way?"

"Yes; the Legislative assembly can do it in a trice."

"Accomplish it, and your fee shall be one hundred dollars, and all contingent expenses paid."

" But the lady—she must petition the Assembly."

"Ah! true," quoth the Major; "and *I* must first petition the *lady*. I will go this moment."

It was twilight; and the lady of the ex-cashier sat alone in the parlor upon the sofa, musing, if the truth *must* be told, not upon the mysterious fate of her liege lord, but upon her young friend who had interested her more deeply of late than everything else, and had in fact so deeply engrossed her affection, that she sometimes forgot her religious duties.

The lovers were together, and their trembling fingers met in silence. She wept, but spoke not, while he unfolded to her the intelligence he had just received, and hinted at the possible means of their being united. " Oh! woman!" he exclaimed, "it may be madness, it may be *crime;* but I *must* tell you how I adore you. I am unworthy of you, but I have struggled hard to deserve your affection. Could you know the depth of my devotion to you, you would pity me. Beautiful, enchanting, endearing woman! you have attracted my fallen spirits upward to virtue, and chained all my affections to yourself. At all times and places, I see and think of you alone. When I was lying at the point of death, and my brow was burning with delirium—even then, I fancied the sunshine of your beautiful eyes shone upon me in my gloomy agonies." * * *

CHAPTER XIX

TAKING A FIGHTING INTEREST.

Mack Black, Mike Killum, and Jake Ropes all swore they would have a fighting interest in the grafted lead. They were regular fighting-cocks, and believed in the supremacy of might. They had a natural thirst for blood and violence, and would pounce upon a lead in contention like wolves upon a carcass. By force or by fraud, one or the other of these biped hyenas had for years managed to get an interest in half the leads in the country. Nothing but the discovery of a lead, by somebody, could ever arouse them from their devotion to the faro banks. They quartered themselves in the most frequented groceries, in diggings where mineral and money were plenty, and there opened their faro banks and roulette tables to decoy and entrap simpletons. If they heard of a mineral discovery, they closed banks and suddenly became *miners*. Their first movement, then, was to foment a dispute amongst the diggers. They were sure to find some one through whom to set up a claim adverse to the discoverer's, no matter how frivolous. Having once got the lead in contention, they would, steathily, while the parties were badly frightened, secure a fighting interest upon their own terms.

Armed to the teeth, these gentlemen made their appearance at Major White's windlass hole, the day after they had heard of Smith & Hawkins' pretentions to the lead.

"I say, stranger," quoth old Mack, looking White in the eye to see if he could be frightened, "I say, old hoss, Smith & Hawkins are a going to play h— with your duck's eggs! They are going to drive you right plum off! We advise you to leave. Bill Hawkins is a hoss. If Bill *says* he'll do a thing, he'll *do* it; now mind I *tell* you."

"Perhaps, gentlemen, you would like to help me defend my diggings?" said the Major with an expression of scorn which was not quite understood.

"We will *shore*," said Black.

"Yes, to the *knife*," added Mike—a little delicate soap-lock, in whose eyes slept the ferocity of a leopard.

"——d——my roaring soul if we *don't* too," added great swaggering Jake.

Old Mike thereupon took hold of the windlass-hook to go down, as if possession were already his.

"Hold!" said the Major. "You may be very nice young men, perhaps—and my friends, and all that; but I do not like your conduct, and I wish you to leave. This is *my* lead—I discovered it. You must not interfere with me. I allow no man to bully *me*. You must leave!"

The three looked at each other, as if hesitating whether or not to throw the Major into the mineral hole.

"You are three," said White, "and I am"—

At this instant Mike began to feel for his pistol. Quicker than thought, White drew and discharged a six-shooter at him, disabling his arm; and instantly wheeled and presented the same formidable weapon at Mack, while Jake took to his heels. The repulse they met with was unlooked for but effectual. They never attempted to jump on the Major with force again; but retreated to Smith & Hawkins' shaft.

"Bill, you can't win at this game," said Black.

"Well, I reckon as how I will, hoss," answered Bill Hawkins, leaning upon his windlass; "why not win?"

"Well," says Mack, "in the first place you can't *drive* White off—he is not *skeery*. Then you can't win at law; you have no show to win; for he will prove by old Buff that he struck the lead first. I know of a trick or two by which you *might* win."

"How is that?" said Bill.

"Oh!" quoth Mike, "that would be telling. What would you give to know?"

The negotiation resulted in Mack's taking a fighting interest of one-half, being Smith's half; with the understanding, that Mack should share Smith's half with Mike and Jake, and that Hawkins should share *his* half with Smith. The suit to be brought in the name of Mack Black and William Hawkins.

CHAPTER XX.

A TRIAL FOR FORCIBLE ENTRY AND DETAINER.

Justice Green's dwelling was a double log cabin in the midst of a vast field of unharvested corn, on which some ten thousand prairie hens were fattening. Before the door there was a single log of firewood, from which several slabs of fuel had been split—also three ox-yokes; a plow of very primitive construction, and a Pennsylvania wagon ironed all over, and of course, too, a tar-bucket slung under the hind axletree. The stable, surrounded with stacks of hay and grain, was also a double log building; and between the logs of which it was built, might be counted the ribs of a pair of hungry old horses, that were starving inside. More phantom hogs "than you could shake a stick at" were flitting and squealing around the premises; they were the kind of hogs known as the wolf breed; either because, from their fleetness and ferocity, they are secure from the depredations of the wolf—or from their wolfish appearance—or because the wolf has no appetite for such pork. They are considered valuable, also, because, when killed, the meat cannot be fly blown, and no more requires salt to preserve it than would an equal quantity of sole leather. The proportions of a genuine wolf-hog are, one-third snout, one-third legs, and the remainder bristles.

The parties, witnesses and counsel in the action of forcible entry and detainer brought by Mack Black and William Hawkins *vs.* James White being all present in court, Mr. Shave, on part of the complainants, read the following complaint:

TRIAL FOR FORCIBLE ENTRY AND DETAINER.

Territory of Wisconsin, } County of Platte.

Mack Black and William Hawkins, of said county, complain unto Pinckney Green, Esq., one of the Justices of the Peace in and for said county, against James White, of said county, for that the said James White, on or about the 15th day of November, A. D., one thousand eight hundred and fifty-one, at the county aforesaid, did, with force and arms, and with a strong hand enter upon and unjustly and illegally detain a certain crevice or range of mineral or lead ore known as the Smith & Hawkins prospect, containing ten acres, the same being on the N. W. quarter of section ——, in town ——, in range——, in Little Blue Rabbit diggings, in said county and territory, contrary to the form of the statute in such case made and provided.
SHAVE & STILL,
Att'ys for Complainants.

To this complaint, and also to the writ, the defendant's attorneys filed the following demurrer:

James White } Before Pinckney
ats. } Green, Esq.
Mack Black, et. al. } In forc. ent. & d.

And the said defendant, by Power & Quibble, his attorneys, comes and defends the wrong and injury, when, etc., and says that the said complaint and writ, and the matters therein contained, in manner and form as the same are above stated and set forth, are not sufficient in law for the said complainants to have or maintain their aforesaid action thereof against the said defendant; and he, the said defendant, is not bound by law to answer the same. And this he is ready to verify; wherefore, by reason of the insufficiency of the said complaint and writ in this behalf, the said defendant prays judgment, and that the said complainants may be barred from having or maintaining their aforesaid action thereof against him, etc.

And the said defendant, according to the form of the statute in such case made and provided, states and shows to the court here the following causes of demurrer to the said complaint and writ, that is to say:

1st. That the complaint purports to be made by Mack Black and William Hawkins; but is subscribed only by Messrs. Shave & Still.

2d. That the complaint does not define on which particular part of the N. W. quarter section described the defendant made the entry complained of.

3d. The complainants do not aver that at the time of the defendant's entry, they, the complainants, were in, or legally entitled to, the possession of said premises.

4th. The complaint charges defendant's entry to have been made in the year 1851—an impossible time.

5th. The writ varies from the complaint, in that the writ charges the entry to have been made in 1841, and the complaint charges the entry to have been made in 1851.

6th. The complaint does not conclude with the usual prayer to the court for a writ.

And also that the said complaint and writ are in other respects uncertain. informal, insufficient, etc.

QUIBBLE & POWER,
Atty's for Defendant.

The demurrer having been fully argued by Messrs. Quibble & Shave, the court was sadly perplexed with doubt. He fidgeted and thumbed the leaves of the statute book and knit his brows. Shave was satisfied that the case was in danger of going by the board. After consulting a moment with Still, an affidavit was prepared and signed by Mr. Black, by which the cause and papers were removed to Jonathan Gosling, Esq., who was present, and immediately took the place of Justice Green.

A removal by the complainants not being provided for by the statute, defendant's counsel excepted.

Gosling was sure to reverse Green's opinion, for it was an axiom with him that Green must *always* be wrong. Gosling was a little, bald-headed, penurious Yankee, in whose eyes a half-dollar looked as large as a cart wheel. He cultivated only six acres of ground, had a barn twice as large as his house, harvested his crops as soon as they were ripe, kept his ox-yokes painted, and greased his wagon wheels with tallow and black-lead.

The demurrer was overruled; and issue being joined on a plea of not guilty, the jury was duly sworn and the examination of witnesses was commenced and not closed before night. Much of the testimony was conflicting, and much of it doubtful, and a great deal more of it entirely irrelevant. For a full report of all the evidence in the case I beg leave to refer the reader to the docket of Esquire Gosling; for Mr. Still carefully filed his own minutes of evidence with the justice that there might be no material variance between the complainant's affidavit for a writ of certiorari, (if a certiorari should be required,) and Justice Gosling's certified return to the District Court. I will here only give the reader the conclusion of a three hours' speech by Mr. Shave for the complainants.

"And now, gentleman of the jury," said Mr. Power, "(for you *are* gentlemen, every one of you,) to be brief— for I promised in the outset to be brief, and it would be an insult to your understanding to argue at great length a case so clear—let me close by drawing your attention to these facts in the case:

1st. That it appears by the testimony of Buff—that an honester man does not breathe the air of heaven, notwithstanding the sneers of counsel and their futile attempts to blacken his character—that Buff and White *did* strike mineral in the hole, (which it has been attempted to be made appear was grafted,) on the 10th day of October; that they not only struck mineral but that they struck it *under* the cap-rock. Whereas the complainants do not even *pretend* that Smith & Hawkins dug before the 21st of October, after it was currently reported that Buff & White had struck the lead. And how do you know, gentlemen of the jury, that they commenced digging on the 21st of October? Who tells you? Who? Why, one of the very men who jumped my client's lead, and who, one week since, openly claimed to own half of it! What! can you believe one word Smith says? Will you believe a man who has the turpitude to offer to swear under such damning *suspicions* of perjury? But suppose they *were* digging on the 21st? What then? the 21st comes *after* the 10th, the day on which *our* discovery was made.

Again it is pretended by opposite counsel that if we *did* make the first discovery the possession has passed out of us by a sale which they allege was made to a Mr. Leech or Mr. Somebody else. Now, in the first place, gentlemen, they have not proved any such sale, (Buff swears that Leech was paid by White for the work he did in the lead;) neither could they; for it existed only in the fruitful imagination of the learned attorney. If Leech dug there he dug for the defendant. But suppose for a moment there *had* been a sale and that the possession become Leech's—how could that sale to Leech vest any right in these complainants? Or suppose for argument's sake, that the right remained in Leech for one week, or one month, and was then returned again to Buff and White—was it not a continuous possession? Could the lead become the complainant's, because, forsooth, they had stolen into one end of it and were in possession during that imaginable point of time in which the possession was passing from Leech back to Buff and White? Such subtleties and sophistry and hair-splitting are an *insult* to a jury. No, no; there was no forfeiture—no abandonment—nothing which should or ever *shall* rob us of our discovery. How long, then, were the diggings unworked by the defendant? Only a few days, and that while the damps were so bad that Buff says he could not and would not risk his life in the shaft —and Leech tried to work there for White and could not— in short, until cold weather. What if their tools were *not* left at the shaft? They were locked up in their cabin that they might be more secure from thieves. Do the complainants grumble because they had not an opportunity to steal our tools as well as our mineral? Again I call your attention to the candor of Buff, who is not a swift witness for *either* party, but speaks out plainly the things that he doth know. He explains why and how long the diggings were unworked; and, mark you, gentlemen, how reluctantly he admits, when asked if the complainant had not tried to *tamper* with him, that this immaculate Mr. Black,—who became a party here, God knows how—[Be careful what you say, Mr. Lawyer, interrupted Mack]—had made a proposition to suborn him as a witness—yes, that was the meaning—to *suborn* him! Gentlemen, how will you reward such virtue as Mack's? Oh! I wish, for the sake of justice, that you were sitting as a jury to try Mr. Black's claim to a cell in the penitentiary; it would do me pleasure, then, to advocate his pretensions. Mr. Flint's evidence corroborates Buff's. Flint is as honest a man as ever suckered a hole, and a miner of great experience; a man who has dug at Nip & Tuck, at Scrabble, at Menominee, at Red Dog, at Whig, at Coon, and almost everywhere else, and he says, that without a declaration of abandonment, a discovery will *not* forfeit in one, or in two, or in three weeks.

Again, you will bear it in mind that it has not been proved, nor *can* it be proved, that the complainants ever went down through the cap rock They never *have* discovered nor been down at *all* through the under body of mineral.

Gentlemen, be just and do right; my client asks no more.

Here Mr. Power closed his speech, being too hoarse to go through with " the pathetic."

THE TRIAL CONTINUED.

Mr. Shave closed on the part of the complainants in substance, as follows:

"Gentlemen, I am done. Our case is before you. Less I could not say in justice to my worthy clients—more I cannot say in justice to you. I see before me a jury of sovereigns—tried men—clear headed men—and some of you practical miners; and I am satisfied. I can read a verdict for the complainants in your honest faces. Gentlemen, I had indeed supposed that this defendant, with money to aid him, with friends to succor and assist him, and with the aid of ingenious and eloquent counsel to defend him, would have made at least a *plausible* defense—that he would have shown some shadow or coloring of right to this mineral range. Alas! fraud is feeble, while truth, eternal truth is mighty and must prevail. The defendant's whole case rests upon the testimony of old Buff, of bogus lead memory—a witness whose very *looks* convict him of perjury—and who has avoided truth so long that he is ashamed to meet it, like the simpleton who avoided meeting the doctor because he was ashamed of not having been sick enough to require his services for so long a time. *Can* such a man tell the truth? To say nothing of the suspicious relations in which he stands to the defendant, look at the man as he stood before you, and say if you can believe him. Why, he is the very incarnation of a lie! What! Do you believe what he swears, that my shrewd and wary client, Mack Black, had the folly to attempt to *suborn* old Buff? False, every word! Mack is not a fool. If the complainants wanted witnesses they would at least have found those whose looks would not bear witness against their words. Why, the old rascal, bad as he is, when cornered on his *voir dire*, admits that White has.

promised to let him have money; but then it is to be a *gratuity*. Oh! yes; of course—a mere *gift*, a *bonus* for his good character! And yet here comes White's attorney and affects to be struck with holy horror at this culprit's statement, that my worthy client, Mack Black, had proposed conveying to him an interest in the diggings, and throws up his arms like a tragedy king, and rolls up the whites of his eyes like a dying duck in a thunder storm! Where, now, do we find this defendant—this spotless Mr. White—this Texan major, whose name is a burlesque on his character—one whom his well paid attorney attempts to hold up in contrast with my excellent and honorable client, Mack Black? Where? Why, assisting old Buff to graft a mineral hole and to swindle an honest stranger from Galena! What? If they had really made a discovery there do you believe, unprincipled as they are, that they would have perpetrated this fraud? or would they not rather have proceded to work out the mineral they had discovered? But suppose they *did* strike mineral on the 19th of October, and that they did sell an actual discovery to Leech, which they afterwards repurchased, did they not leave the ground for *weeks* without a tool upon it? was it not abandoned? forfeited? while Smith & Hawkins were, and had been for a long time, working the east end of the range, as everybody knew, without an objection raised by this defendant? No, gentlemen, there was no discovery—and that the real consideration for the two hundred and fifty dollars which White paid to Leech was the adjustment and settlement of a prosecution which Leech was about to commence against that pair of worthies for swindling him out of nine thousand dollars! There, you have it; and if Mr. Anthony Power could be sworn he would *tell* you so."

("No, I wouldn't," muttered Power.)

"How easy for the defendant to have left tools on the ground during his three weeks' absence as a sign of continued occupancy? No, no; White never *thought* of going back to dig until he heard that Smith & Hawkins were raising mineral. What says the witness Clay, who has badgered more holes in the mines than there are in half an acre of honeycomb, and raised more *thousands* of mineral than Flint has raised *pounds?* He says that the damps *never* prevent working a shaft in October; and that every one who abandons his mineral lot for more than seven days, weather and health permitting him to dig, and carries away his windlass and all his tools, absolutely forfeits his ground."

"Gentlemen of the jury; as you love honesty and industry, and as you abhor rascality and fraud, I conjure you, in behalf of my clients, to find for them, as I have no doubt but you will, a verdict that they have restitution of the premises, and the lead of which this defendant has wrongfully robbed them."

When Counsellor Shave had closed the case, Justice Gosling waked up, and the jurors yawned, and every soul wished himself at home sleeping in a warm bed, like the thirteen white haired urchins that were snoring in one corner of the court room. The brass clock tolled four. The fire in the huge chimney was nearly extinct. This was a circumstance favorable to a speedy verdict. The jury was given in charge of a constable, and everybody else went out to await their verdict. The weather had suddenly changed and grown cold as hell reversed. From thawing to freezing, the change was almost instantaneous. The frost penetrated and chilled everything. It stung like fire. All caloric seemed annihilated. In five minutes the earth began to crack as if it would be shivered; and the teeth chattered so that no man could articulate; and the five hundred and odd spectre swine lying between the double log stables, squealed and growled and groaned as if they were in the agonies of death. The prairie hens upon the stacks were so torpid that they might have been brushed off with a stick.

Some were trying to listen at the door and learn what the jury was about. The cold was increasing and became intolerable. Buff and Black went to get their horses where they had left them tied in the cold to nibble at some prairie hay. There stood the horses with their fixed glassey eyes, each with a wisp of hay in his mouth, but the poor creatures were frozen as solid as marble. Buff felt his face freezing and clapped his hands to his jaws; at the touch his whiskers snapped and broke off like icicles; and finally every man was obliged to start and run for his dear life; and the jury was left hanging just as the dim sun arose with his crimson dogs and scowled across the bleak prairie ridges.

What made it so cold? Why, old Jack Frost has been up in the region of Bear Lake hunting for polar bears; and being agent (long before Dousman was) of the American Fur Company, he had business down at St. Louis; and that happened to be the very night in which old Jack bound on his skates and started down the Mississippi. The surface of the great river congealed under the breath of his nostrils, and the trees were incrusted with hoar frost as he skimmed the ringing ice with giant strides, making everything sparkle and crack again. The freightened steamboats stood still, the engines were palsied—and shivering nature did homage to the king of winter. Frost and steam were twin brothers, born of old mother Chaos; but they never could agree from their infancy. Jack was always a practical joker—would turn out at night to cut up shines and break things—and the loafer is just as full of his pranks as ever—while his twin brother, Steam, has taken to hard work of late years, is very industrious, and makes a great deal of money; but Steam will sometimes get too high and give everybody in his way a blowing up. If Jack would take to labor and work with his brother, the pair would make business ache. What a pair of miners they would make! Jack with his beetle and wedges to crack open the shell of the earth, and his brother to raise the mineral out of the openings.

CHAPTER XXI.

BURIED ALIVE.

Mr. Buff and Mr. Black started for Blue Rabbit by the way of Potawattamie diggings, where they stopped to liquor at a doggery. They took a hand at "poker" with the "boys," who were there assembled. By the middle of the afternoon, the weather had greatly moderated, and the sun was encircled with a "circumstance," that denoted a coming storm. Buff and Mack were by this time pretty "essentially corned." Towards night they started off across the prairie for Little Blue, Buff taking with him a glass flask, on one side of which the thirteen stars and the face of Washington were moulded. The flask was filled with "sweet scented Rock river." The snow had for two hours been showering down like feathers, and almost blinded our travellers. The tops of the grass were not visible in the road, and this negative sign was the only indication where the path was; night was coming on, and no *land* in sight; and still they had some miles to go. The wind arose, and began to beat the snow about in whirling eddies, and pile it in drifts. The darkness thickened, the cold increased, and the storm howled around them with frightful fury. Their limbs were benumbed with cold. Scarcely able to stand against the tempest, they soon lost their way.

"Buff, let us kick in the snow," said Black, "and try to find the ruts in the road."

"Why, Mack, my legs are so cold I couldn't *feel* a rut with my foot; and I am afeared to get down on my knees to feel with my hands, *least* I couldn't get up again."

"Gracious God! what a tempest! It is as dark as a nigger's pocket—and the storm beats so I can't stand. What shall we do?"

"Mack, we shall never get through this snowbank; we shall be covered—drifted over—out of sight, in five minutes. Let us turn to the left and run before the wind. Lord! how I shiver!"

"Well, Buff, put out the flask, and let us take a horn first, to keep us from freezing. We would hate to be left here frozen like our horses *is*, or like Lot's wife—standing monuments of the cold. D—— all lawsuits, I say."

They turned and ran before the wind, they knew not whither, for half an hour. By this time the liquor they had swallowed began to take effect; they came to a ravine in which were some hazel bushes a little protected from the storm. They crept away in these bushes to lay down to rest.

"Ugh! ugh!" uttered Mack, puffing and blowing, "I'm clean out of—breath—I'm fairly—ugh! ugh! fairly wind-broken—I am. Give me some—ugh! ugh!—some liquor, Buff."

"I shan't," stammered Buff, "do—hic—any such thing—hic—Mack.—You've got more—hic—more liquor than you can carry now. Old Buff will take the—hic—remainder."

"The h— you will!" roared Mack, making a grasp for the flask. They instantly clenched and fought like dogs, rolling over and over down the drifted ravine; when all at once—thrash!—they fell, locked together, to the bottom of a mineral hole forty feet deep.

Were they not killed? inquires the reader.

Killed? no! how can you kill a man who is drunk? They *deserved* to be killed—but I must confine myself to facts; they were only badly stunned, and it was some time before they knew what sort of a fix they were in. They soon felt the influence of the warmer atmosphere into which they had tumbled.

Their intoxication was banished by fear.

"The Lord bless me!" groaned Buff, "who is here? Oh! oh! oh! dear!—Oh! is this—Oh! is this Mack?'

Mack groaned; "Oh! get off of me! get up! I'm killed—I'm dead. Where in h— are we? Who sells liquor here."

"We have," said Buff, groping and feeling about him, "we have not exactly got home to our papa's down below; but we are part way there—we are in a mineral hole."

They soon fell asleep. When they awoke in the morning and looked up and saw how deep a hole they were in they were much alarmed. They felt the gnawings of hunger and wanted, more than all, whisky, their habitual stimulus.

They halloed a few times; but that was hopeless. Mack next took his bowie knife and commenced digging holes with it in the sides of the shaft for steps to climb up by. After carving out and climbing up one step after another for about twenty feet, the earth in the sides of the shaft under him caved and he fell to the bottom with the precipitated mass, in which Buff was nearly buried. The increased diameter of the hole as well as its conical form forbade any further attempts to get out by cutting new steps in the sides. They sat down in despair, constantly treated with the fall of the mass of earth above them

Another night came—a horrible night—and morning dawned upon their sleepless eyes. Buff began to show symptoms of *delirium tremens*. Their hunger became intolerable. Mack found a toad burrowing in the hole. He tried to conceal it from Buff, but did not succeed. Buff begged and cried like a child for a part of it, and his comrade, not yet utterly selfish, divided the reptile with him.

Does the reader inquire how the toad came there? I do not know. The toad *was* there. Toads have been found imbedded in solid rock, but I cannot account for their being found there.

Another day came and brought no hopes. Mack's lips were parched with thirst, and his tongue was turning black, and he blasphemed most horribly. Buff was foaming with madness. Their cheeks grew hollow and their beards had grown long and squalid.

Another morning dawned and they had fallen into a state of drowsiness. Buff dreamed that he was invited to sit down at a table on which was spread " the great sheet filled with all manner of birds and beasts and creeping things" cooked, which was let down to St. Peter by the four corners; and as he fancied he was carving a roasted elephant he smiled and smacked his parched lips.

Another day dawned, but no hope; they would sit and cry like children; then they would blaspheme and curse the very name of heaven; and then they would cry again but shed no tears. That night a horrible idea had seized the mind of each, that the other designed to murder and feast upon him. Each burrowed a hole with his skeleton fingers behind him; in these holes they crept and sat all night, gnashing their teeth and glaring at each other, their rabid eyes shining like fire. At last Mack darted out like a spider from his hole and pounced upon his imaginary foe. He caught Buff by the wrist of the right hand and broke his right arm at the elbow across his knee, and with his bowie knife separated it from the stump, and with the shriek of a devil incarnate swung it over his head. That moment the whole impending mass of earth caved and slumped in with a noise like muffled thunder.

What became of the rest of your scoundrels? perhaps the reader inquires. Jake Ropes has been severely punished —and Mike Killum has fled westward with the brand of Cain upon his forehead. Mr. Leech served a year's apprenticeship in the penitentiary, then went to Texas where he received an appointment as Secretary of the Territory; Smith & Hawkins are still in the diggings."

CHAPTER XXI.

TERRITORIAL LEGISLATION.

The Legislative Assembly was in session at Madison; for even then Belmont collapsed, and the principal evidence of its existence was to be found in the recorded deeds of city lots. Balbec and Palmyra and Babylon are in ruins, and scarcely a vestige of Belmont remains.

"*Tempus edox rerum,*"—a sad sentiment which Virgil must have written expressly for the epitaph of Belmont. An old moss-covered house was described as standing by the side of the Dutchman's little dog, so the traveller will always find the East Platte Mound standing by the side of the ruins of Belmont—a monument as ancient as any city (of its age) can boast of.

Madison, the city of the four lakes, is destined to be famous hereafter. When? When Wisconsin shall become an affluent and populous State; and when Milwaukee, sitting like Venice and looking out upon her fleets of merchantmen, shall be the emporium of a trade richer than the dreams of avarice. Will this be? It will, and that quickly

What were the members assembled for? Three dollars a day and mileage. What had they to do? Attend the calling of the roll, and answer aye or no, and do as little mischief as possible and go home. Still, there was a great show of business to be done. There were speeches to be made; and the members lounging in the lobby were whispering, and bargaining, and log-rolling, like hackneyed politicians.

The lobby was thronged.

"Gentlemen, one and all," said Col. Too-Slick, a perpendicular young Whig member from the county of Platte, "gentlemen, I invite you all to oysters and wine at my room this evening at nine o'clock. I have a little matter to talk over with you which interests one of my constituents."

The invitation was not declined, and all were at supper.

"Can't head the old fox off—Tyler will save him," said Dane, finishing a plate of oysters.

"Pshaw!" said Iowa, breaking the neck off a bottle of champagne, "we know a little of the royal game of goose if we *can't* corner him. I'll wager my financial character that he don't make three jumps more upon the board before he is cornered." "Ha! ha!" quoth Brown, "you might as well attempt to get to windward of Old Nick. The only chance is to run the 'old White Horse' after him." "These oysters are very good—very good—very good," said Crawford, nibbling a cracker; "but pray, Col. Too-Slick, to what scene of corruption are we indebted for this excellent supper? No draught upon the Treasury designed, I hope?" "Well, the long and short of the business is," said Col. Too-slick, pulling his whiskers and speaking in a confidential under tone, "there is a lady in our county"—

"Here's to her health!" said Iowa, drinking, "here's to her health, God bless her!—anything that I can do for a woman "—

"The loveliest woman," continued Col. Too-Slick, "you ever saw. Well, the amount of the business is, her husband has just been tried and sentenced to the penitentiary in Michigan."

"And wants a divorce," interrupted Sauk. "Why don't she petition in Chancery? Colonel, we ought to discourage these applications."

"But," continued Col. Too-Slick, "her husband has so much influence there is danger of his getting a pardon."

"Aye, aye," quoth Racine, "in a case of emergency like that I would pass a bill for the relief of Mrs. Potiphar if she couldn't wait."

"No," quoth Milwaukee with vast gravity, "never keep a woman in suspense if you can avoid it, especially one who has the good sense to try what virtue there is in oysters and champagne. Gentlemen, I consider this an elegant and injured woman."

"Gentlemen," said Iowa, rising, "please fill up your glasses. Are you ready?"

"All ready."

"Here's to Col. Too-Slick's lovely constituent. We will find her in fresh husbands as long as she will find us in fresh oysters."

The toast was drunk with great enthusiasm. Poor Mary little knew of all this rudeness at her expense.

"Suppose," said Crawford, "you append the bill to my bill for legalizing the official acts of Paul Lynch and making him a good, sufficient justice of the peace for the year 1836?"

"Agreed," said Col. Too-Slick. "It will then read 'a bill to legalize the official acts of Paul Lynch and for other purposes therein named.'"

"Yes," said Iowa, "that *therein named* often covers greater multitude of legislative sins than charity. It means 'too black to index.' And, by way of rider, my Kamonistoquire mill-dam bill."

"And mine," quoth Sauk, "for the protection of catfish above the forks of the Pecatonica."

The bill was framed as incongruous in its parts and provisions as an inventory of the contents of Noah's ark. It passes the committee like physic—went through its third reading in triumph—and was concurred in—and became a law.

CHAPTER XXIII.

CONCLUSION

At the same hour did Major White receive intelligence that the jury had finally returned a verdict in his favor and that his betrothed was divorced. In ten days he was united to Mary.

> And oh! let Mary be her name,
> It hath a sweet and gentle sound,
> At which no glories dear to fame
> Come crowding round;
> But which the dreaming hour beguiles
> With holy thoughts and household smiles.

Since then the Major and his lady has visited Clocktown and the home of Mary's youth in Massachusetts—visited Saratoga, and elegantly furnished a fine new house with superb furniture—not forgetting the cradle. Their children are both vaccinated. The Major himself has been born again and is one of the most eminent saints in the church and his lead is still unexhausted. When the nascent star of Wisconsin shall glisten in the constellation of states, *his* political star will be in the ascendant. Major James White, late of the army of Texas, still firmly believes that he was even more fortunate when he *won a wife* than when he *struck a lead.*

www.ingramcontent.com/pod-product-compliance
Lightning Source LLC
Chambersburg PA
CBHW021943160426
43195CB00011B/1209